Macroeconomic policy analysis

Macroeconomic policy analysis

Open economies with quantity constraints

Michael Amos
Harvard University

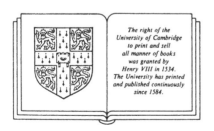

CAMBRIDGE UNIVERSITY PRESS

Cambridge
New York   New Rochelle   Melbourne   Sydney

CAMBRIDGE UNIVERSITY PRESS
Cambridge, New York, Melbourne, Madrid, Cape Town, Singapore, São Paulo, Delhi

Cambridge University Press
The Edinburgh Building, Cambridge CB2 8RU, UK

Published in the United States of America by Cambridge University Press, New York

www.cambridge.org
Information on this title: www.cambridge.org/9780521115742

First published 1988
This digitally printed version 2009

A catalogue record for this publication is available from the British Library

Library of Congress Cataloguing in Publication data
Amos, Michael
    Macroeconomic policy analysis: open economies with quantity
    constraints / by Michael Amos.
    p. cm.
    Bibliography: p.
    ISBN 0-521-34387-9
    1. Monetary policy – Mathematical models. 2. Credit control –
Mathematical models. 3. Macroeconomics – Mathematical models.
I. Title.
HG230.3.A47 1988
339.5′3 – dc19   88-10844

ISBN 978-0-521-34387-9 hardback
ISBN 978-0-521-11574-2 paperback

To My Mother and Sister

Contents

Tables

Preface

This book presents a modern approach to macroeconomic policy analysis. The analytical framework is non-Walrasian. The disaggregation of the government into the treasury and the central bank, and the specification of the behavior of households, firms, and the central bank as intertemporal optimizers are among the distinguishing features of the book. Its primary purpose is to introduce policy makers, economists, and advanced students to a modern theoretical framework which could serve as the basis for macroeconomic policy analysis and to introduce the concept of public sector rationing in asset markets. The detailed treatment of credit rationing regimes makes portions of the book particularly relevant to economies where the interest rate is rigid. The following policy instruments are discussed: open market operations, bond-financed change in the level of government consumption, incomes policies, interest rate regulations, interest rate targets, exchange rate targets, and money supply targets. In addition, the effects of adjustments in prices (exchange rate, bond price, and so forth) on the government's budget and the economy are highlighted.

The unique specification of the intertemporal behavior of the central bank makes intervention in asset markets (the bond market and the foreign exchange market) endogenous in the short run and allows for the introduction of the concept of public sector rationing in the asset markets. Rationing in asset markets, due to interest rate regulations or central bank optimization problems, alters the effectiveness of the treasury's policies in the short run. This is demonstrated under different regimes characterized by rationing in asset markets and unemployment.

The models presented can easily be extended to take into account both institutional and economic structures of all types of economies (small and large) and the particular needs of the policy analyst before empirical implementation.

Acknowledgments

My greatest debt of gratitude in preparation of this book is to R. Bryce Hool, who introduced me to non-Walrasian macroeconomics and provided detailed comments on several drafts of this book. In addition, for their many useful comments, I wish to thank Irma Adelman, who read an earlier version of Chapters 2 and 3; Polly Reynolds Allen, who read Chapter 5; Volker Bohm, who read the final manuscript; and Egon Neuberger, who read an earlier draft. I alone bear the responsibility for any remaining errors.

Acknowledgment is also due to Colin Day and the editorial and production staff at Cambridge University Press, whose desire for excellence has resulted in a far better book than would otherwise have been achieved.

CHAPTER 1

Introduction and background

There are essentially two views about the way a modern economy functions: the classical view and the Keynesian view. The classicists assume that prices contain all the relevant information about market conditions and that they adjust infinitely fast so that trade takes place at the equality of demand and supply in every market; thus, producers and consumers need be concerned only with price signals. This view may correctly describe the way a simple economy with centralized markets operates, but it ignores the complex institutional structure of modern economies and the informational problems of decentralized markets, which prevent instantaneous adjustment of prices. Labor contracts, interactions between unions and firms (lags induced by wage negotiations), wage–price guidelines, absence of an auctioneer in most markets, absence of futures markets for all goods, sorting and incentive effects of prices, and so forth prevent instantaneous adjustments in prices. Admittedly, any model that attempts to capture in detail the institutional structure of a modern economy is likely to be so complex as to render the model useless. However, as a first simplifying step, instantaneous price adjustments can be ruled out; this is the point of departure for the Keynesians. Once instantaneous price adjustments are ruled out, some markets may not clear at the prevailing prices, which leads to quantity adjustments (e.g., involuntary unemployment and involuntary inventory accumulation). When quantity adjustments are required, consumers and producers become concerned with quantity signals in addition to price signals. It was the contributions of Patinkin (1956), Clower (1965), Leijonhufvud (1968), and Barro and Grossman (1971) that brought into focus the distinction between these conflicting views about how a modern economy functions.

Patinkin, in a partial-equilibrium model, traced the source of involuntary unemployment to insufficient commodity demand. Firms that are unable to sell their profit-maximizing level of output (considering only price signals) revise their production plans (taking quantity signals into account), thereby causing a reduced demand for labor input (involuntary unemployment). Patinkin thus disassociated involuntary unemployment from the level of real wages. In Patinkin's model all that is

1

required to produce involuntary unemployment is that the wage–price constellations be such that there is insufficient demand for products.

Clower, in a partial-equilibrium model, examined the microfoundations of the Keynesian consumption function. He contended that the inclusion of income as an argument of the consumption function can be justified by examining the behavior of households that are unable to realize their conventional supply of labor. The conventional supply (and demand) functions of the households are derived under the assumption that the only constraint on choice is the value of initial endowments. In the terminology of Clower these demand functions are called *notional demands*. Notional demands depend on price signals, endowments, and expectations rather than on income because, in the conventional analysis of household behavior, labor supply is a choice variable (i.e., endogenous). However, when there are quantity constraints in addition to endowment constraints, then the households' demands reflect these quantity constraints. When there is involuntary unemployment, households face a constraint on labor supply, which leads to a revision of the demands they express in other markets. Clower called these recalculated demands *effective demands*. Effective demands differ from notional demands in that the former depend on prices, endowments, expectations, and *quantity constraints*, whereas the latter depend only on prices, endowments, and expectations. The distinction between effective demands and notional demands is a crucial distinguishing feature of Keynesian analysis, and it is the direct consequence of ruling out instantaneous price adjustments. This point was highlighted by Leijonhufvud.

Leijonhufvud (1967, 1968) argued that the classical notional-demand theory is invalid because it assumes that prices adjust infinitely fast to clear markets. On the other hand, all that is needed for the Keynesian analysis to be correct is the assumption that the speed of price adjustment is finite. In other words, price rigidity is not a central issue for Keynesian effective-demand analysis. Leijonhufvud contends that in reality, because of informational problems and liquidity constraints, quantities may adjust faster than prices.

Barro and Grossman (1971) combined and extended the models of Patinkin (1956) and Clower (1965), drawing on the insights of Leijonhufvud (1967, 1968), to obtain a general equilibrium model of a closed economy. Barro and Grossman assumed that quantities adjust faster than prices and considered a short enough period of time so that prices could be viewed as rigid. Because prices are assumed to be rigid in the short run, there can be excess supply or excess demand on a market. Barro and Grossman examined two extreme cases: general excess supply (for goods and labor) and general excess demand (for goods and labor). They explored the implications of the fact that when demand functions are effective demands, markets become interdependent directly through quantities. Because during a depression the labor demand depends on the firm's sales constraint, the one-to-one relationship between real wages and employment is removed. Barro and Grossman also pointed out the apparent asymmetry in previous Keynesian macroeconomic models of a depressed economy that treat consumption as a function of income (price and quantity) while ignoring the effect on labor demand of the constraint on the supply of goods (labor demand is assumed to be notional). In addition, their analysis of the case of general excess demand (for labor and capital) suggests an interesting possible outcome. When households are constrained (rationed) in their purchases of goods, their demands for unconstrained goods are effective demands. In particular, labor supply will be a function of the goods ration. In this case, households may reduce their labor supply, thus reducing the level of output and further exacerbating the imbalance in the goods market (a case for intervention). These conceptual developments generated much interest in the microfoundations of Keynesian macroeconomics and the policy implications of short-run price rigidities. (See Drazen 1980 for a survey of the literature.)

The Keynesian models that have appeared in the literature since 1971 share with the previous Keynesian models the assumption of finite price adjustment. However, most of the recent models are more rigorous than pre-Barro–Grossman models in the sense that demand and supply functions are derived from the optimization problems of households and firms. This approach has eliminated the inconsistencies of earlier Keynesian models (e.g., treating demand for labor as notional in a depressed economy). The current Keynesian methodology for economic analysis emphasizes that the initial economic environment (who is rationed in which market) conditions the response to policy. For this reason the economy is classified in terms of *regimes*. For example, in an economy with two markets (labor and product) and rigid prices each market can have excess demand or excess supply; so there are four possible regimes. The specification of a model leads to a classification of possible regimes, and policy response is conditional on the current regime of the economy. The researchers who employ this methodology have attempted to disassociate their work from the pre-1971 Keynesian methodology by using as a portion of their titles such terminology as neo-Keynesian; non-Walrasian (to distinguish it from Walrasian general equilibrium theory, which assumes instantaneous price adjustment); temporary equilibrium with rationing (to distinguish it from the Hicksian temporary equilibrium); disequilibrium; a model with price rigidities, and others. The term *disequilibrium* has been a source of some confusion, and the more recent contributions avoid using it. In fact, *the Keynesian models are equilibrium models.*

Two concepts of equilibrium are currently used in economics. In the classical analysis, equilibrium refers to equality between notional demands and supplies in all markets, which is the idea of Walrasian equilibrium. In Keynesian analysis, equilibrium refers to a state in which the decisions of (optimizing) agents are mutually consistent; this state is called a non-Walrasian equilibrium. A non-Walrasian equilibrium does not require equality of demands and supplies in all markets. For example, consider a situation in an economy with two markets (product and labor). The firms are constrained in the product market, and the households are constrained in the labor market. In this case, the firms have effective demands for labor that reflect their sales ration, and the households have effective demands for goods that reflect their labor ration. This economy is in a non-Walrasian equilibrium when the households express effective demands for goods C, based on their labor ration n, which induce the firms to employ the same amount of labor n. In other words, we have a non-Walrasian equilibrium when price and quantity signals regenerate themselves.

1.1   Context of this book

Antecedent non-Walrasian, open-economy models have focused on the policy implications of rationing in product and labor markets. To date, the policy implications of rationing in asset markets, despite its obvious relevance, has not been explored.[1] This book examines the policy implications of two types of rationing in asset markets, making distinction between private-sector and public-sector rationing in such markets.

1.2   Private-sector rationing in asset markets

Private-sector rationing in an asset market occurs when the firms and/or households are unable to acquire their notional demand for an asset. Credit rationing is an example of this type of rationing. In Chapters 2–4

---

[1] The first draft of this book was copyrighted in 1983. When this manuscript was in its final stages, I became aware of a working paper by John Cuddington and Per Olov Johansson (1986) on fiscal deficit-reduction programs in the presence of credit rationing. Their analysis is restricted to the case in which firms are rationed in the credit market. For a model of commercial-bank portfolio selection and banking policies in a small, open economy, see Amos (1986).

of this book the focus of the analysis is on domestic policy effectiveness when credit is rationed. Credit rationing is a widely observed phenomenon in all types of countries[2] and it will be demonstrated that it has general equilibrium effects which can alter qualitatively the effectiveness of macroeconomic policies.

The model developed to explore the policy implications of credit rationing is an extension of Dixit (1978). Dixit models a small, open economy under a fixed-exchange-rate regime. This economy is populated by households, firms, and the government. Households are intertemporal optimizers, choosing current consumption, leisure, and domestic money balances. Firms do not have a budget constraint and are concerned only with maximizing current-period profits. The government's behavior is exogenous; that is, no budget constraint is specified. There is one input (labor), one output, one asset (domestic money), and no inventory accumulation.

This model goes beyond Dixit's in several dimensions: (1) It incorporates an interest-bearing asset that permits the analysis of credit-rationing regimes; (2) it distinguishes between bond-financed fiscal policy and monetary policy, which requires that we take into account the treasury's budget constraint; and (3) it takes account of the effects of various policies on inventory accumulation (investment). This is achieved by specifying an intertemporal optimization problem for firms. The specification of the model developed here also draws on the recent models of Hool (1980) and Bohm (1981), both of which describe closed economies.

---

[2] Instantaneous adjustments of asset prices may be prevented by the institutional structure of the developing and developed economies, the regulation of the banking sector, imperfect competition in the banking sector, and imperfect information.

In most developing economies, the government regulates the interest rate. Portugal, Cyprus, Malta, Turkey, Egypt, Jamaica, Colombia, and Peru are only a few of the many countries with administered interest rates in 1986. (This information was provided by the government officials of the respective countries.) According to a recent study by the International Monetary Fund (1983) government officials of the developing countries state various reasons for interest-rate regulations: The control of interest rates in conjunction with direct or indirect allocation of loanable funds permits the government to reduce the cost of financing its national debt, reduce monopolistic or oligopolistic profits of the commercial banking sector, stimulate priority sectors, promote competition in productive industries, and move the economy towards a "better" equilibrium.

In developed economies, the recent trend is toward deregulation of the banking sector. However, some developed economies continue to administer some interest rates (e.g., Sweden). In developed economies that have deregulated the banking sector (e.g., the United States), rationing in the credit market may still occur due to the finite speed of interest-rate adjustment, default risk, regional usury laws, optimization behavior of commercial banks in markets with imperfect information (see Stiglitz and Weiss 1981), and so forth.

Hool (1981) is an extension and generalization of Malinvaud (1977), with an economy populated by firms, households, and the government. In this model, firms do not hold bonds, and they have a one-period optimization problem of maximizing current profits. Households are intertemporal optimizers, choosing current consumption and a portfolio of money and bonds. The government, which is a consolidation of central bank and treasury, does not optimize. Its policy variables are related within the budget constraint, expenditures being financed by issuing domestic assets (money and bonds). Hool's formulation is useful because it allows a distinction between a pure (bond-financed) fiscal policy and a pure monetary policy (open-market operations). The specification of the behavior of households and the treasury's budget constraint in this book is based on Hool's model.

Bohm (1981), drawing on the work of Sondermann (1974), builds on the models of Barro and Grossman (1976) and Malinvaud (1977). In Bohm, the economy is populated by households and firms, both of which are intertemporal optimizers. Households choose labor supply, consumption level, and domestic money balances. Firms choose the level of planned production and money holdings, which implies a choice of inputs: labor and goods (inventory accumulation). Domestic money is the only financial vehicle for interperiod transfer of wealth. The specification of the behavior of firms in this book is based on Bohm's model, but the menu of assets held by firms is extended to include domestic bonds. This extension allows analysis of the impact of various policies on current supplies of goods and employment through their effects on the firm's disposable wealth in addition to price and wage channels.

1.3   Public-sector rationing in asset markets

Public-sector rationing in an asset market occurs when there is a conflict between a primary objective of a public authority and its portfolio selection. To date, this type of rationing has not been recognized by economists. An example of this type of rationing is the portfolio selection of the central bank (e.g., optimal foreign-asset reserves) subject to its stabilization policies (e.g., exchange-rate target). The central bank may have excess demand for an asset that is not expressed on the market because, if it were expressed, it would result in an unacceptable change in asset prices. For example, consider a situation in which the domestic central bank has an excess demand for foreign assets and its primary concern is domestic inflation. In this environment the central bank may not express its notional demand for assets on the market because purchases of foreign assets might lead to exchange-rate depreciation which exacerbates the domestic inflation problem. In Chapter 5 the focus of the analysis is on the implications of the central bank's portfolio selection and stabilization policies for the efficacy of the treasury's policies.

The model in Chapter 5 extends the model of earlier chapters in several dimensions: (1) It allows managed floating exchange rate and interest rate regimes, which requires augmenting the model with a central bank; (2) it emphasizes the role of asset markets in exchange-rate determination, which requires incorporating multiple assets (domestic money, domestic bonds and foreign assets) into the analysis; and (3) it focuses the analysis on public-sector rationing in asset markets.

1.4   The plan of this book

The plan of this book is as follows. Chapters 2–4 examine domestic policy effectiveness under fixed exchange rate regimes with credit rationing. In Chapter 2 households are rationed in the labor market and firms are rationed in the credit market. In Chapter 3 households are simultaneously rationed in the labor and credit markets, while firms are not rationed in any market. In Chapter 4 both households and firms are rationed in the credit market. Chapter 5 examines the effectiveness of the treasury's policies when the central bank is rationed in the asset markets. The summary of the results of Chapters 2 to 5 is contained in Chapter 6. The appendix discusses monetary and fiscal policy effectiveness under a perfectly flexible interest rate regime.

CHAPTER 2

Firms rationed in the credit market

This chapter examines domestic-policy effectiveness in a small, open economy with price rigidities. What distinguishes this analysis from previous, related open-economy models[1] is the possibility of rationing in the credit market due to interest-rate rigidity. Thus, it is a natural extension of existing neo-Keynesian open-economy models, which up to now have concentrated only on the policy implications of rationing in product and labor markets. The importance of this extension needs little elaboration. Credit rationing is a widely observed phenomenon in all types of economies and has important general equilibrium effects. For example, a firm that cannot raise the level of credit it wants may reduce its planned production and therefore its demand for labor. Also, it may reduce its planned inventory accumulation, increasing its current supply of goods. On the other hand, a household that is rationed in the credit market may revise its demand for goods. Thus, the effect of macroeconomic policy on the supply of goods and the demand for labor and goods is conditioned, in part, by its effect on the availability of credit.

The basic model developed in this chapter can be employed for analyzing all types of regimes with rationing in the credit market (i.e., regimes characterized by excess demand or excess supply of credit). The temporary equilibrium under consideration is characterized by firms rationed in the credit market and households rationed in the labor market. The analysis of the case in which households are simultaneously rationed in the credit and labor markets is the subject of Chapter 3; and in Chapter 4, we allow for simultaneous rationing of firms and households in the credit market.

2.1 The model

The setting is a small, open economy that produces a composite commodity by employing domestic labor and previously produced goods. The domestic agents are separated into four groups: firms, households,

---

[1] See Chapter 1 for the context of this book.

the treasury, and the central bank. There are five goods: labor services, produced goods, domestic money, domestic bonds, and foreign money.

Domestic firms are buyers in the labor market and net sellers in both the product market and the bond market. Domestic households are buyers in the product market, sellers in the labor market, and net buyers in the bond market. The domestic treasury is a buyer in the product market and the issuer of domestic assets (money and bonds). The exchange rate e is fixed, and there is no capital mobility.

Under a fixed-exchange-rate regime, the central bank may have excess demand or excess supply of foreign currency. The analysis of the policy implications of the imbalance in the foreign-exchange market requires a separate treatment, which is discussed in detail in Chapter 5. For the regimes considered in Chapters 2–4, it is assumed that the central bank has sufficient foreign-currency reserves to maintain the exchange rate.

The domestic nominal wage w, the domestic nominal bond price q, and the foreign nominal price of goods p^* are rigid in the short run. Transportation costs are negligible, and arbitrage in goods insures that they sell for the same price (adjusted for the exchange rate) in all countries. That is, $p = ep^*$, where p is the domestic nominal price of goods. Henceforth $p^* = 1$, so that $p = e$.

The small-country assumption permits the ignoring of all foreign repercussions; so only the behavior of domestic agents is elaborated. Also, although the economy is populated by many firms and households, for simplicity a representative firm and household are utilized.

2.2 The treasury

The treasury selects the level of its expenditures and the method of financing them. Government expenditures can be financed by issuing domestic assets. A treasury bond is a perpetuity that pays one unit of domestic currency per period. The treasury's budget constraint is

$$eG = M^g - M_o^g + qB^g - (q + 1)B_o^g, \qquad (2.1)$$

where G is real government purchases of goods; M^g and M_o^g are the final and initial stocks of domestic money, respectively; and B^g and B_o^g are the final and initial stocks of domestic bonds, respectively (B_o^g is also the interest payment on outstanding debt).

2.3 The household

The representative household has a two-period planning horizon. It chooses current consumption C and leisure H and plans for future consumption. There are no future markets, and the household holds domestic currency M and domestic bonds B.

Given that prices are rigid, we must distinguish between the household's desired demands and its realized transactions. In conventional microeconomics, the household's demand functions are obtained under the assumption that the only constraint on choice is the value of initial endowments. In the terminology of Clower (1965) these demand functions are called *notional demands*. The household's notional demands are the solution to the following optimization problem:

$$\text{Maximize} \quad V(C, M, B, Z - L)$$
$$\text{Subject to} \quad eC + M + qB = wL + M_o + (q + 1)B_o, \quad (2.2)$$

where $V(\ )$ is a strictly quasi-concave derived utility function,[2] M_o and B_o are the initial assets, Z is total time, and L is labor supply $(Z - L = H)$. The notional demands are

$$C(e, w, q),$$
$$M(e, w, q),$$
$$B(e, w, q),$$

and $\quad H(e, w, q) = Z - L(e, w, q),$ $\hfill (2.3)$

where here and henceforth the dependence on initial assets is suppressed. Also, we assume throughout that all goods are normal and are gross substitutes.

In the event that the household is unable to realize its notional demand in some market, it has to recalculate its utility-maximizing choice of other goods. Clower (1965) calls these recalculated demands *effective demands*. Effective demands reflect quantity constraints imposed on the household by the market. For example, when labor demand n is less than notional labor supply L, effective supply of labor equals labor demand (this is called the short-side rule).[3] In this case, the effective demands are

---

[2] Expectations about future prices and quantity rations are reflected here, as in Dixit (1978), in the elasticities of the demand functions. For an alternative treatment of expectational variables, see Neary and Stiglitz (1983) or Amos (1981).

[3] As in the previous related models, we have assumed that exchange is voluntary and that the market is "efficient". That is, trading is not imposed on any agent, and all mutually advantageous trading opportunities are exploited. These assumptions jointly imply that the agent on the short-side of the market (the buyer if there is excess supply and the seller if there is excess demand) is not rationed. This rules out the possibility of simultaneous excess demand and excess supply on a market. Thus, transactions in each market will equal the minimum of aggregate demand and aggregate supply on that market.

$$\tilde{C}(e, w, q, n),$$
$$\tilde{M}(e, w, q, n),$$
$$\tilde{B}(e, w, q, n),$$

and $\quad \tilde{H} = Z - \tilde{L} = Z - n.$ (2.4)

It is assumed that

$$\tilde{C}_e < 0; \quad \tilde{C}_w, \tilde{C}_q, \tilde{C}_n > 0;$$
$$\tilde{B}_q < 0; \quad \tilde{B}_w, \tilde{B}_e, \tilde{B}_n > 0;$$
$$\tilde{M}_e, \tilde{M}_w, \tilde{M}_q \quad \text{and} \quad \tilde{M}_n > 0.$$ (2.5)

In general, when prices are rigid, the household may face a quantity constraint (ration) in any market. However, for a small, open economy, a common assumption is that no rationing takes place in the traded-goods market; that is, any discrepancy between domestic aggregate demand and aggregate supply of the traded good will be made up by international trade.[4] In addition to this assumption, for the case considered in this chapter, the household is assumed to be a net buyer in the bond market. This, in conjunction with the assumption that there is an excess supply of bonds, implies that the household is not rationed in the credit market (the short-side rule).

2.4 The firm

The representative firm has preferences over domestic assets M^* and B^* and over future production Y^{**}. This reflects a one-period lag in production, which makes M^*, B^*, and Y^{**} alternative means of interperiod transfer of wealth. The production lag implies that the stock of goods produced domestically Y_o^* is the result of production decisions made in the previous period. Production is achieved by employing domestic labor E^* and previously produced goods used as input I^*. Thus, the current-period supply of goods Y^* is the difference between the initial stock of goods and the goods used as input for future production, $Y^* = Y_o^* - I^*$.

When the firm is not rationed in any market, its optimization problem is

---

[4] Dixit (1978), and Neary (1980) make a similar simplifying assumption. I also agree with Malinvaud (1980, page 95), who has pointed out that the smallness of an economy does not always preclude it from being rationed in the product market. The possibility of the imbalance in the goods market must be taken into account in empirical tests of rationing in asset markets. However, the small country assumption has proven to be a very useful simplifying assumption for the purpose of introducing new models and highlighting new channels through which macroeconomic policy can effect the domestic economy.

Maximize $V^*(Y^{**}, M^*, B^*)$

Subject to $TC(e, w, Y^{**}) + M^* + qB^* = (q + 1)B_o^* + M_o^* + eY_o^*$,

(2.6)

where $V^*(\ )$ is strictly quasi-concave derived utility function (see note 2, page 10), and $TC(\ )$ is a cost function that is convex in Y^{**}.

The notional-demand functions of the firm, which are the solution to (2.6) are

$$Y^{**}(e, w, q),$$
$$M^*(e, w, q),$$
$$B^*(e, w, q),$$
$$I^*(e, w, q) = Y_o^* - Y^*(e, w, q),$$

and $\quad E^*(e, w, q).$ (2.7)

As before, we assume that all goods (including inputs) are normal and gross substitutes.

Given that prices are rigid, the firm may be rationed as a seller in the goods and bond markets and as a buyer in the labor market. However, as in the case of the household, the small-country assumption is used to rule out the possibility of rationing in the goods market. Also, for the case under consideration, it is assumed that there is unemployment; so the firm is not rationed in the labor market. When the firm is rationed as a seller in the bond market, its effective demands are

$$\tilde{Y}^{**}(e, w, q, b),$$
$$\tilde{M}^*(e, w, q, b),$$
$$\tilde{E}^*(e, w, q, b),$$
$$\tilde{I}^*(e, w, q, b) = Y_o^* - \tilde{Y}^*(e, w, q, b),$$

and $\quad \tilde{B} = B_o^* - b,$ (2.8)

where b is the bond ration (i.e., the firm's effective supply of bonds). It is assumed that

$$\tilde{Y}_e^{**}, \tilde{Y}_w^{**} < 0; \quad \tilde{Y}_q^{**}, \tilde{Y}_b^{**} > 0;$$
$$\tilde{M}_e^*, \tilde{M}_w^*, \tilde{M}_q^*, \tilde{M}_b^* > 0;$$
$$\tilde{I}_w^*, \tilde{I}_q^*, \tilde{I}_b^* > 0; \quad \tilde{I}_e^* < 0; \quad \tilde{Y}_w^*, \tilde{Y}_q^*, \tilde{Y}_b^* < 0; \quad \tilde{Y}_e^* > 0;$$

and $\quad \tilde{E}_e^*, \tilde{E}_q^*, \tilde{E}_b^* > 0; \quad \tilde{E}_w^* < 0.$ (2.9)

2.5 Comparative statics

For the case under consideration, the household is rationed as a seller in the labor market, and the firm is rationed as a seller in the bond market.

The household's income-constrained effective demands for goods, money, and bonds are $\tilde{C}(e, w, q, n)$, $\tilde{M}(e, w, q, n)$, and $\tilde{B}(e, w, q, n)$, where n is the labor ration. Effective labor supply is $\tilde{L} = n$. The firm is unable to sell its notional supply of bonds; this is reflected in its planned production $\bar{Y}^{**}(e, w, q, b)$ and money holdings $\bar{M}^{*}(e, w, q, b)$, where b is the bond ration. The firm's effective demands for labor and goods input are $\tilde{E}^{*}(e, w, q, b)$ and $\tilde{I}^{*}(e, w, q, b)$. So the effective supply function for goods is $\tilde{Y}^{*}(e, w, q, b) = Y_o^{*} - \tilde{I}^{*}$.

The household's effective demand for bonds (conditional on its labor ration) implies a bond ration for the firm. On the other hand, the firm's effective demand for labor is conditional on its bond ration. When the effective demand for labor is consistent with the household's effective demand for bonds, the domestic economy is in equilibrium. In other words, this regime is in a temporary equilibrium with rationing when the labor ration and the bond ration regenerate themselves. The equilibrium of this regime is characterized by

$$\tilde{L} = \tilde{E}(\dot{e}, \dot{w}, \dot{q}, \dot{b}) = n, \qquad (2.10)$$

and

$$B^g - \tilde{B}(\dot{e}, \dot{w}, \dot{q}, \dot{n}) = \tilde{B}^{*} = \tilde{B}_o^{*} - b. \qquad (2.11)$$

Any discrepancy between domestic supply and demand for goods is made up by international trade. In this sense the goods market clears continuously. The balance of trade in real units is

$$T = \tilde{C}(\dot{e}, \dot{w}, \dot{q}, \dot{n}) + G - \tilde{Y}^{*}(\dot{e}, \dot{w}, \dot{q}, \dot{b}). \qquad (2.12)$$

Solving for B^g in (2.11) and substituting for it in the government's budget constraint, we obtain

$$eG = M^g - M_o^g + q\tilde{B}(\dot{e}, \dot{w}, \dot{q}, \dot{n}) - qb - (q + 1)B_o^g + qB_o^{*}. \qquad (2.13)$$

To examine the effect of changes in government spending G, money supply M^g, and prices e, w, and q on employment n, the firm's bond ration b, and the balance of trade T, we take the total differential of equations (2.10), (2.12), and (2.13) to obtain

$$\begin{bmatrix} 1 & \tilde{Y}_b^{*} & -\tilde{C}_n \\ 0 & -\tilde{E}_b^{*} & 1 \\ 0 & q & -q\tilde{B}_n \end{bmatrix} \begin{bmatrix} dT \\ db \\ dn \end{bmatrix} =$$

$$\begin{bmatrix} (\tilde{C}_e - \tilde{Y}_e^{*}) \, de + (\tilde{C}_w - \tilde{Y}_w^{*}) \, dw + (\tilde{C}_q - \tilde{Y}_q^{*}) \, dq + dG \\ \tilde{E}_e^{*} \, de + \tilde{E}_w^{*} \, dw + \tilde{E}_q^{*} \, dq \\ dM^g + q\tilde{B}_w \, dw + (q\tilde{B}_e - G) \, de + (\tilde{B} + q\tilde{B}_q + \tilde{B}^{*} - B_o^g) \, dq - e \, dG \end{bmatrix}. \qquad (2.14)$$

The determinant of the matrix of the coefficients is

$$A^{-1} \equiv -q(1 - \tilde{B}_n \tilde{E}_b^*) < 0. \qquad (2.15)$$

That the determinant A^{-1} is negative follows from the reasonable assumption that all "marginal propensities to consume" are less than one.[5]

2.6   Differential effects of monetary and fiscal policies

The government budget constraint (i.e., $eG = M^g - M_o^g + qB^g - (q + 1)B_o^g$) makes monetary, fiscal, and price adjustment policies interdependent. Total differentiation of the government budget constraint yields

$$e \, dG + G \, de = dM^g + q \, dB^g + (B^g - B_o^g) \, dq. \qquad (2.16)$$

A bond-financed increase in government spending (i.e., $edG = qdB^g > 0$ and $dM^g = de = dq = 0$) reduces the firm's current-period disposable wealth and leads to lower planned production ($\tilde{Y}^{**}$ is a normal good). This reduces the demand for inputs, causing an increase in the current supply of goods and a decrease in employment.[6]

$$db/dG = e\bar{A} < 0; \quad dn/dG = e\bar{A}\tilde{E}_b^{*+} < 0; \quad d\tilde{Y}^*/dG = e\bar{A}\tilde{Y}_b^{*-} > 0. \qquad (2.17)$$

The increase in government purchases worsens the balance of trade directly, while the increase in the current supply of goods, in conjunction with lower consumption (due to lower employment), improves the balance of trade. However, it will be shown that the net effect is a deterioration of the balance of trade.

$$\begin{aligned} dT/dG &= 1 - e(\tilde{Y}_b^{*-} - \tilde{C}_n^+\tilde{E}_b^{*+})\bar{A} \\ &= 1 - e(\tilde{Y}_b^{*-} - \tilde{C}_n\tilde{E}_b^*)(-q + q\tilde{B}_n\tilde{E}_b^*)^{-1} \end{aligned} \qquad (2.18)$$

The balance of trade deteriorates if

$$-e(\tilde{Y}_b^{*-} - \tilde{C}_n^+\tilde{E}_b^{*+}) + (-q + q\tilde{B}_n^+\tilde{E}_b^{*+}) = \Psi < 0. \qquad (2.19)$$

---

[5] $\tilde{B}_n\tilde{E}_b^* = (q/w)(\tilde{B}_n) \cdot (w/q)(\tilde{E}_b^*).$

[6] Typically, an increase in employment does not imply a reduction in unemployment. In the models discussed in this book this distinction does not arise. However, in more complicated models, the effect on both employment and unemployment should be assessed.

Substitution from the household's and the firm's budget constraints yields[7]

$$\Psi = -\overset{\pm}{\tilde{M}_b^*} - \overset{\pm}{\tilde{M}_n}\overset{\pm}{\tilde{E}_b^*} < 0. \tag{2.20}$$

An expansionary monetary policy (i.e., $dM^g = -q\ dB^g > 0$ and $dG = de = dq = 0$) reduces the supply of government bonds and enables the firm to increase its borrowing. This increases the firm's current-period disposable wealth and leads to higher demand for labor and lower current supply of goods.

$$db/dM^g = -\bar{A} > 0; \quad dn/dM^g = -\bar{A}\overset{\tilde{+}}{\tilde{E}_b^*} > 0; \quad dY^*/dM^g = -\bar{A}\overset{\tilde{-}}{\tilde{Y}_b^*} < 0. \tag{2.21}$$

The reduction in the current supply of goods, in combination with the increased consumption due to higher levels of employment, leads to a deterioration of the balance of trade.

$$dT/dM^g = \bar{A}(\overset{\tilde{-}}{\tilde{Y}_b^*} - \overset{\pm}{\tilde{C}_n}\overset{\pm}{\tilde{E}_b^*}) > 0. \tag{2.22}$$

2.7 The relationship between the real wage and employment

The effective demand for factors of production reflects the firm's bond ration $\tilde{E}^*(e, w, q, b)$ and $\tilde{I}^*(e, w, q, b)$. An increase in the real wage (with a fixed exchange rate), in the absence of the spillover effect from the bond market, leads to lower employment as the firm substitutes the relatively cheaper goods input for the labor input. However, as the real wage increases, the firm's bond ration may change because the household's effective demand for bonds reflects its labor ration $\tilde{B}(e, w, q, n)$. (Recall that $B^g - \tilde{B} = B^* - b$.) Therefore, the net effect on demand for factors of production is, in general, ambiguous. This, in combination with the uncertain effect on consumption demand $\tilde{C}(e, w, q, n)$, makes the effect on the balance of trade ambiguous.

[7] Partial differentiation of the household's budget constraint with respect to n yields

$$e\tilde{C}_n + \tilde{M}_n + q\tilde{B}_n = w. \tag{A.1}$$

Multiplying A.1 by $\tilde{E}_b^*$ and rearranging terms yields

$$e\tilde{C}_n\tilde{E}_b^* = -\tilde{M}_n\tilde{E}_b^* - q\tilde{B}_n\tilde{E}_b^* + w\tilde{E}_b^*. \tag{A.2}$$

Partial differentiation of the firm's budget constraint with respect to b yields

$$w\tilde{E}_b^* + \tilde{M}_b^* = q + e\tilde{Y}_b^*. \tag{A.3}$$

Multiplying A.3 by -1 and rearranging terms yields

$$-e\tilde{Y}_b^* = q - w\tilde{E}_b^* - \tilde{M}_b^*. \tag{A.4}$$

Substitution from A.2 and A.4 in Ψ yields

$$\Psi = -\tilde{M}_b^* - \tilde{M}_n\tilde{E}_b^* < 0.$$

$$db/dw = -q\bar{A}(\overset{\pm}{\bar{B}}_w \qquad + \overset{\pm}{\bar{B}}_n\overset{-}{\bar{E}}{}^*_w)$$
$$= -qA(\text{direct effect} + \text{spillover effect})$$
$$dn/dw = -q\bar{A}(\overset{-}{\bar{E}}{}^*_w \qquad + \overset{-}{\bar{E}}{}^*_b\overset{\pm}{\bar{B}}_w)$$
$$= -qA(\text{direct effect} + \text{spillover effect})$$
$$dT/dw = (\overset{\pm}{\bar{C}}_w - \overset{-}{\bar{Y}}{}^*_w) - q\bar{A}(\overset{\pm}{\bar{C}}_n\overset{-}{\bar{E}}{}^*_w + \overset{\pm}{\bar{C}}_n\overset{-}{\bar{E}}{}^*_b\overset{\pm}{\bar{B}}_w - \overset{-}{\bar{Y}}{}^*_b\overset{\pm}{\bar{B}}_w - \overset{-}{\bar{Y}}{}^*_b\overset{\pm}{\bar{B}}_n\overset{-}{\bar{E}}{}^*_w)$$
$$= (\text{direct effects}) + (\text{spillover effects}) \qquad (2.23)$$

In the event that the direct effect of an increase in the nominal wage on the bond, labor, and goods markets exceeds its indirect (spillover) effects, the bond ration increases, labor demand decreases, and the balance of trade deteriorates (all goods are gross substitutes).

$$db/dw > 0; \quad dn/dw < 0; \quad dT/dw > 0. \qquad (2.24)$$

2.8   Devaluation, employment, and the balance of trade

The treasury's budget constraint (i.e., $eG = M^g - M^g_o + qB^g - (q + 1)B^g_o$) requires that a devaluation of the domestic currency (an increase in e) be accompanied by a change in M^g or B^g or G or q. Thus, there are several cases to consider, depending on the method of financing the devaluation.

Case 1: Money-financed devaluation

A money-financed devaluation (i.e., $de = (1/G)dM^g > 0$ and $dB^g = dG = dq = 0$) leads to an increase in labor demand through two channels. As the domestic price level increases (recall that $p = e$), the firm substitutes the relatively cheaper labor input for the goods input. Also, the firm's bond ration increases (higher employment leads to higher demand for bonds by the household); this leads to a further increase in employment and to an increase in the demand for goods used as input (the firm's disposable wealth increases).

$$db/de = -q\bar{A}(\overset{\pm}{\bar{B}}_e + \overset{\pm}{\bar{B}}_n\overset{-}{\bar{E}}{}^*_e) > 0,$$
$$dn/de = -q\bar{A}(\overset{\pm}{\bar{E}}{}^*_e + \overset{\pm}{\bar{E}}{}^*_b\overset{\pm}{\bar{B}}_e) > 0. \qquad (2.25)$$

The net effect on the balance of trade is uncertain. On the supply side, the effect of the increase in the demand for bonds may offset the effect of devaluation on the demand for goods as input. In addition to the uncertainty about the level of current output, there is uncertainty about the effect on aggregate demand due to the increase in employment, which may offset the decrease in consumption due to the higher price of goods.

$$dT/de = (\bar{\tilde{C}_e} - \overset{+}{\tilde{Y}_e^*}) + \overset{+}{\tilde{S}_e}$$
$$= \text{(direct effects)}$$
$$+ \text{(spillover effects from the labor and bond markets)}, \tag{2.26}$$

with $\tilde{S}_e = -q\bar{A}(\bar{\tilde{C}_n}\overset{+}{\tilde{E}_b^*}\overset{+}{\tilde{B}_e} + \overset{+}{\tilde{C}_n}\overset{+}{\tilde{E}_e^*} - \bar{\tilde{Y}_b^*}\overset{+}{\tilde{B}_n}\overset{+}{\tilde{E}_e^*} - \bar{\tilde{Y}_b^*}\overset{+}{\tilde{B}_e})$.

Therefore, the balance of trade will improve as a result of a devaluation if the direct effects on consumption and the current supply of goods exceed the spillover effects via the bond and the labor markets.

Case 2: Devaluation and reduction in government spending

The impact of a devaluation of the domestic currency accompanied by a reduction in government spending (i.e., $de = (-e/G)\,dG > 0$ and $dM^g = dB^g = dq$) on the labor ration and bond ration is identical to that of a money-financed devaluation; this is because, in both cases, there is no direct effect on the firm's disposable wealth. In both cases, the devaluation directly affects the firm's demand for labor (inputs are substitutes), which in turn affects the supply of credit by the household. The increase in the supply of credit feeds back on the labor market, further increasing the demand for labor. However, when the devaluation is accompanied by a reduction in government spending, its impact on the balance of trade differs quantitatively and potentially qualitatively from money-financed devaluation. The reason is that the reduction in government spending reduces the balance of trade directly, and so it increases the likelihood of an improvement in the balance of trade as a result of the devaluation.

$$dT/de = (\bar{\tilde{C}_e} - \overset{+}{\tilde{Y}_e^*} - (\overset{+}{G/e})) + \overset{+}{\tilde{S}_e}$$
$$= \text{(direct effects)} + \text{(spillover effects)}. \tag{2.27}$$

It should be noted that the spillover effects from the labor and bond markets (i.e., $\tilde{S}_e$) are the same for cases 1 and 2.

Case 3: Bond-financed devaluation

Alternatively, a devaluation may be accompanied by an increase in the stock of bonds (i.e., $de = (q/G)\,dB^g > 0$, $dG = dM^g = dq = 0$). In this case, the effect of the devaluation on employment and the balance of trade is ambiguous. The increase in the price of goods leads to an increase in demand for labor (as in the previous cases). However, the increase in the supply of bonds by the government may offset the increased demand for bonds by the household. So the net effect on the firm's bond ration, and thus the net effect on demand for factors of production, is uncertain. The uncertainty about the effect on the demand for inputs makes the effect on consumption demand and the current supply of goods, and thus on the balance of trade, ambiguous.

$$db/de = -q\bar{A}(\bar{B}_n \overset{\pm}{\tilde{E}^*_e} + \overset{\pm}{\tilde{B}_e}) + \bar{A}G$$

$$= \text{(effects of devaluation with a fixed stock of bonds)}$$

$$+ \text{(effect of the change in the stock of bonds)}.$$

$$dn/de = -q\bar{A}(\overset{\pm}{\tilde{E}^*_b}\overset{\pm}{\tilde{B}_e} + \overset{\pm}{\tilde{E}^*_e}) + \bar{A}\overset{\pm}{\tilde{E}^*_b}G$$

$$= \text{(effects of devaluation with a fixed stock of bonds)}$$

$$+ \text{(effect of the change in the stock of bonds)}.$$

$$dT/de = (\overset{\approx}{\tilde{C}_e} - \overset{\pm}{\tilde{Y}^*_e}) + \overset{\pm}{\tilde{S}_e} - \bar{A}G(\overset{\approx}{\tilde{Y}^*_b} - \overset{\pm}{\tilde{C}_n}\overset{\pm}{\tilde{E}^*_b})$$

$$= \text{(direct effects of devaluation)}$$

$$+ \text{(spillover effects with a fixed stock of bonds)}$$

$$+ \text{(spillover effects due to the change in the stock of bonds)}.$$

$$(2.28)$$

It should be noted that the spillover effects induced by the change in the stock of bonds increase the likelihood of an improvement in the balance of trade as a result of a devaluation (crowding-out effect).

Case 4: Devaluation and a change in the bond price

A devaluation may be accompanied by a change in the bond price (i.e., $de = (1/G)(B^g - B^g_0) dq$ and $dM^g = dB^g = dG = 0$). If the treasury is a net buyer of bonds (i.e., $B^g - B^g_0 < 0$), then devaluation requires a decrease in the bond price.[8] On the other hand, if the treasury is a net seller of bonds (i.e., $B^g - B^g_0 > 0$), then an increase in the bond price is needed. The net effect of devaluation accompanied by a change in the bond price on employment, the bond ration, and the balance of trade depends only in part on the sign of $B^g - B^g_0$. An increase in q leads to a substitution of goods for bonds, reducing the firm's bond ration. The reduction in the firm's bond ration will reduce its demand for factors of

---

[8] In practice, it may not be possible to fully finance a devaluation by a decrease in the price of bonds.

production, while the increase in q increases the demand for factors of production (disposable-wealth effects); so the net effect on demand for factors of production as a result of a change in q is uncertain. Also, the change in the household's labor ration feeds back on the bond market, making the net effect on the firm's bond ration ambiguous.

$$db/de = -q\bar{A}(\overset{\pm}{\tilde{B}_n}\overset{\pm}{\tilde{E}_e^*} + \overset{\pm}{\tilde{B}_e}) + (-q\bar{A})[G/(B^g \overset{?}{-} B_o^g)](\overset{\pm}{\tilde{B}_n}\overset{\pm}{\tilde{E}_q^*} + \overset{\pm}{\tilde{B}_q})$$

$$= \text{(effects of devaluation with a fixed bond price)}$$
$$+ \text{(effects of a change in the bond price)}$$

$$dn/de = -q\bar{A}(\overset{\pm}{\tilde{E}_b^*}\overset{\pm}{\tilde{B}_e} + \overset{\pm}{\tilde{E}_e^*}) + (-q\bar{A})[G/(B^g \overset{?}{-} B_o^g)](\overset{\pm}{\tilde{E}_b^*}\overset{\pm}{\tilde{B}_q} + \overset{\pm}{\tilde{E}_q^*})$$

$$= \text{(effects of devaluation with a fixed bond price)}$$
$$+ \text{(effects of a change in the bond price)} \qquad (2.29)$$

If the treasury is a net buyer of bonds (i.e., $B^g - B_o^g > 0$), devaluation is accompanied by a higher bond price [recall that $de = (B^g - B_o^g)(1/G)\, dq > 0$]. In this case, if the direct effect of an increase in the bond price dominates its indirect effects on the labor and bond markets (i.e., $-\tilde{B}_q > \tilde{B}_n\tilde{E}_q^*$ and $\tilde{E}_q^* > -\tilde{E}_b^*\tilde{B}_q$), employment will increase, but the effect on the bond ration is ambiguous.

If the treasury is a net buyer of bonds (i.e., $B^g - B_o^g > 0$), the spillover effect of a change in q (i.e., $\tilde{E}_b^*\tilde{B}_q$) complements the effect of devaluation on the labor market, whereas the direct effect of q on the bond market (i.e., $\tilde{B}_q$) complements the effect of devalaution on the bond market. In this case, if the direct effect of a change in the bond price exceeds its indirect effects on the labor and bond markets, the bond ration increases, though the net effect on employment is uncertain.

The effect of devaluation accompanied by a change in the bond price on the balance of trade is ambiguous. In addition to the direct and spillover effects of devaluation, there is the direct and spillover effects of the change in the bond price on the demand and supply of goods.

$$dT/de = (\overset{\pm}{\tilde{C}_e} - \overset{\pm}{\tilde{Y}_e^*}) + [G/(B^g \overset{?}{-} B_o^g)](\overset{\pm}{\tilde{C}_q} - \overset{\pm}{\tilde{Y}_q^*}) + \overset{\pm}{\tilde{S}_e}$$

$$+ q\bar{A}[G/(B^g \overset{?}{-} B_o^g)](\overset{\pm}{\tilde{Y}_b^*}\overset{\pm}{\tilde{B}_n}\overset{\pm}{\tilde{E}_q^*} - \overset{\pm}{\tilde{C}_n}\overset{\pm}{\tilde{E}_q^*} + \overset{\pm}{\tilde{Y}_b^*}\overset{\pm}{\tilde{B}_q} - \overset{\pm}{\tilde{C}_n}\overset{\pm}{\tilde{E}_b^*}\overset{\pm}{\tilde{B}_q})$$

$$= \text{(direct effects of devaluation)}$$
$$+ \text{(direct effects of the change in the bond price)}$$
$$+ \text{(spillover effects of devaluation)}$$
$$+ \text{(spillover effects of the change in the bond price)}.$$

$$(2.30)$$

If the bond price is reduced (i.e., when $B^g - B_o^g < 0$), consumption demand decreases as the household substitutes bonds for goods (i.e., $\tilde{C}_q$

> 0). Also, the reduced bond price leads to a decrease in the firm's disposable wealth, causing lower planned production. With lower planned production, fewer inputs are needed. Thus, the current supply of goods increases (recall that $\tilde{Y}^* = Y_o^* - \tilde{I}^*$ and $\tilde{Y}_q^* < 0$). If the spillover effects of devaluation and the reduction in the bond price [refer to (2.30) for dT/de] do not dominate the direct effects, the balance of trade improves as a result of the devaluation. However, if an increase in the bond price is needed (i.e., when $B^g - B_o^g > 0$), the direct effect of the increase in the bond price may offset the direct effect of the devaluation on the goods market. Thus, even with small spillover effects, there is uncertainty about the net effect on the balance of trade.

CHAPTER 3

Households rationed in the credit market

This chapter extends the model of Chapter 2 by allowing for simultaneous rationing of the household in both the credit and labor markets. As before, the small-country assumption is used to rule out the possibility of rationing in the traded-goods market. In addition, we assume that firms are net buyers in the bond market. This, in combination with the short-side rule, implies that firms are not rationed in the credit market. Also, because there is unemployment, firms are not rationed in the labor market.

The analysis of domestic-policy effectiveness in this environment is important because, in practice, demand for many durable goods (e.g., automobiles) is likely to be very sensitive to the household's credit ration. Despite the assumption that the household does not store goods (i.e., views all goods as perishable), the analysis in this chapter is suggestive of the impact of domestic policies on the interest-sensitive sectors that produce traded goods in a small, open economy. The model of this chapter is essentially the same as that in Chapter 2, so only a brief description of economic agents follows.

3.1   The model

Recall that the small, open economy produces a traded composite commodity by employing labor and goods inputs. Purchasing-power parity and the assumption of a rigid world price (normalized to one) implies that the exchange rate e is the domestic price level. The exchange rate is fixed, and there is no capital mobility.

The government's real purchases of goods G are financed by issuing domestic assets B^g and M^g. A treasury bond is a perpetuity paying one unit of domestic currency per period. The treasury is not rationed in any market. Its budget constraint is

$$eG = M^g - M^g_0 + qB^g - (q + 1)B^g_0. \tag{3.1}$$

There is a one-period lag in production. The firm chooses between alternative means of interperiod transfer of wealth: planned production Y^{**}, money M^*, and bonds B^*. Production is achieved by employing

21

labor E^* and goods inputs I^* in such a way as to minimize total cost. The current supply of goods Y^* is the difference between the initial supply of goods Y_o^* and the goods used as input, $Y^* = Y_o^* - I^*$. For the case under consideration, the firm is assumed to be a net buyer in the bond market. This, in conjunction with an excess supply of labor, implies that the firm, which is producing a traded good in a small, open economy, is not rationed in any market. The firm's notional demands are

$$Y^{**}(e, w, q),$$
$$M^*(e, w, q),$$
$$B^*(e, w, q),$$
$$I^*(e, w, q) = Y_o^* - Y^*(e, w, q),$$

and $E^*(e, w, q).$ (3.2)

Recall that all goods are normal and are gross substitutes.

The household is assumed to be rationed as a seller of bonds and labor services; so it has effective demands for goods $\hat{C}$ and money $\hat{M}$, which reflect its rations. The effective demands are

$$\hat{C}(e, w, q, n, b),$$
$$\hat{M}(e, w, q, n, b),$$
$$\hat{L} = n,$$

and $\hat{B} = B_o - b,$ (3.3)

where n is the labor ration and b the bond ration (i.e., effective net supply of bonds by the household).

The domestic economy is in equilibrium when the quantity rations regenerate themselves. This equilibrium is characterized by

$$\hat{L} = E^*(\dot{e}, \bar{w}, \dot{q}) = n,$$ (3.4)

and

$$B^g - B^*(\dot{e}, \dot{w}, \bar{q}) = \hat{B} = B_o - b.$$ (3.5)

The small-country assumption implies that the domestic agents are not rationed in the goods market. The balance of trade measures the excess of domestic aggregate demand $(\hat{C} + G)$ over domestic aggregate supply Y^*. The balance of trade in real units is

$$T = \hat{C}(\bar{e}, \dot{w}, \dot{q}, \dot{n}, \dot{b}) + G - Y^*(\dot{e}, \bar{w}, \bar{q}).$$ (3.6)

Solving for B^g in (3.5) and substituting into the government budget constraint yield

$$eG = M^g - M^g_o + qB^*(\dot{e}, \dot{w}, \dot{q}) - qb + qB_o - (q + 1)B^g_o. \tag{3.7}$$

Total differentiation of (3.4), (3.6), and (3.7) gives the following system of equations:

$$\begin{bmatrix} 0 & 0 & 1 \\ 1 & -\hat{C}_b & -\hat{C}_n \\ 0 & q & 0 \end{bmatrix} \begin{bmatrix} dT \\ db \\ dn \end{bmatrix} =$$

$$\begin{bmatrix} E^*_e\, de + E^*_w\, dw + E^*_q\, dq \\ (\hat{C}_e - Y^*_e)\, de + (\hat{C}_w - Y^*_w)\, dw + (\hat{C}_q - Y^*_q)\, dq + dG \\ -e\, dG + (qB^*_e - G)\, de + dM^g + (B^* + \hat{B} + qB^*_q - B^g_o)\, dq + qB^*_w dw \end{bmatrix}. \tag{3.8}$$

3.2 Monetary and fiscal policies and the balance of trade

Given that the firm has a notional demand for labor, $E^*(\dot{e}, \dot{w}, \dot{q})$, and a notional supply of goods, $Y^*(\dot{e}, \dot{w}, \dot{q})$, monetary and fiscal policies will have no effect on employment and the supply of goods (as long as prices are rigid).

An open-market purchase of bonds (i.e., $dM^g = -q\, dB^g > 0$ and $dG = dq = de = 0$) increases the supply of credit. In response to this, the household, which has an excess supply of bonds, will reduce its stock of bonds. This increases the disposable wealth that can be allocated to the consumption of goods and money holdings. As the household's consumption demand increases, the balance of trade deteriorates; that is,

$$dT/dM^g = (1/q)\,\overset{+}{\hat{C}_b} > 0. \tag{3.9}$$

On the other hand, an expansionary fiscal policy (i.e., $e\, dG = q\, dB^g > 0$ and $dM^g = de = dq = 0$) increases the supply of bonds, further crowding out the household from the credit market. This leads to a decrease in the demand for goods (disposable wealth decreases), which improves the balance of trade. However, as long as the marginal propensity to consume out of disposable wealth is less than one, the decrease in consumption demand will be less than the increase in government purchases. Therefore, the net effect is a deterioration of the balance of trade:

$$dT/dG = 1 - (e/q)\overset{+}{\hat{C}_b} > 0, \tag{3.10}$$

where $(e/q)\hat{C}_b$ is the marginal propensity to consume out of disposable wealth.

3.3   Devaluation, employment, and the balance of trade

An increase in the exchange rate (with $G\ de = dM^g$) leads to a substitution of labor ($E_e^* > 0$) for the relatively expensive goods input ($I_e^* < 0$). As the demand for goods used as input decreases, the current supply of goods increases ($Y^* = Y_0^* - I^*$). Also, the firm will substitute bonds ($B_e^* > 0$) and money ($M_e^* > 0$) for planned production ($Y_e^{**} < 0$). The firm's increased demand for bonds permits the household to reduce its stock of bonds. The increase in employment, in combination with higher bond sales (by the household), leads to higher demand for goods ($\hat{C}_n$, $\hat{C}_b > 0$), worsening the balance of trade, while the increase in the price of goods lowers consumption demand and leads to an increase in the supply of goods ($\hat{C}_e < 0$; $Y_e^* > 0$). Thus, the net effect on the balance of trade is uncertain.

$$dT/de = \overset{-}{\hat{D}_e} + \overset{+}{\hat{S}_e}$$

$$= \text{(direct effects)} + \text{(spillover effects)}, \tag{3.11}$$

where $\hat{D}_e = (\overset{-}{\hat{C}_e} - \overset{+}{Y_e^*})$ and $\hat{S}_e = (\overset{+}{\hat{C}_n}\overset{+}{E_e^*} + \overset{+}{\hat{C}_b}\overset{+}{B_e^*})$.

In the event that the direct effect of devaluation on consumption and the current supply of goods exceeds the spillover effects of devaluation (via the bond and labor markets) on consumption demand, the balance of trade improves ($dT/de < 0$).

The effect on employment of alternative methods of financing a devaluation is easily determined because under this regime the firm has a notional demand for labor, $E^*(\acute{e}, \bar{w}, \acute{q})$. Therefore, a devaluation accompanied by a reduction in government spending, an increase in the stock of bonds, or an increase in the bond price leads to an increased demand for labor (goods are substitutes). If a devaluation is accompanied by a decrease in the bond price [i.e., $B^g - B_0^g < 0$ and $G\ de = (B^g - B_0^g)\ dq > 0$], the effect on employment is uncertain; this is because the reduction in the bond price leads to the substitution of bonds for planned production by the firm, causing a reduction in demand for inputs. Thus, the effect of a decrease in the bond price may offset the effect of the devaluation on demand for labor. The effect of a devaluation, accompanied by a change in the bond price on employment is

$$dn/de = \overset{+}{E_e^*} + \overset{+}{E_q^*}[G/(B^g \overset{?}{-} B_0^g)]$$

$$= \text{(effect of devaluation)} + \text{(effect of the change in } q\text{)}. \tag{3.12}$$

The effect on the bond supply ration is also easily determined. The firm's notional demand for bonds is $B^*(\acute{e}, \bar{w}, \bar{q})$.

The household's bond ration is $b = B^*(e, w, q) + B_o - B^g$. Therefore, an increase in exchange rate with $dq = dB^g = 0$ unambiguously leads to an increase in the household's bond ration. An increase in the exchange rate accompanied by a decrease in the bond price (i.e., $B^g - B_o^g < 0$) leads to an increase in the bond ration as the firm substitutes planned production and money for bonds. If an increase in the bond price is required, the net effect on the bond ration is ambiguous. The effect of devaluation accompanied by a change in the bond price on the bond ration is

$$db/de = \overset{+}{B_e^*} + \bar{B_q^*}[G/(B^g \overset{?}{-} B_o^g)]$$
$$= \text{(direct effect of devaluation)}$$
$$+ \text{(direct effect of the change in the bond price)}.$$
$$(3.13)$$

A bond-financed devaluation (i.e., $de = (q/G) dB^g > 0$ and $dM^g = dG = dq = 0$) has an ambiguous effect on the household's bond ration because the increase in the stock of bonds may offset the increase in the demand for bonds due to the substitution of bonds for planned production by the firm.

$$db/de = \overset{+}{B_e^*} - (G/q)$$
$$= \text{(direct effect of devaluation)}$$
$$+ \text{(direct effect of the change in the stock of bonds)}.$$
$$(3.14)$$

A devaluation accompanied by a reduction in government spending (i.e., $de = (-e/G) dG > 0$ and $dM^g = dB^g = dq = 0$) is more likely to improve the balance of trade than a money-financed devaluation. This is because a reduction in government spending improves the balance of trade directly.

$$dT/de = [\bar{D}_e - (G/e)] + \overset{+}{\hat{S}_e}$$
$$= \text{(direct effects)} + \text{(spillover effects)}. \qquad (3.15)$$

A devaluation accompanied by an increase in the stock of bonds (i.e., $de = (q/G) dB^g > 0$ and $dM^g = dG = dq = 0$) affects the balance of trade through several channels. The direct effects are identical to the case of money-financed devaluation [i.e., $(\hat{C}_c - Y_c^*)$]. However, there is another spillover effect (in addition to S_e) due to the increase in the stock of bonds, which decreases consumption demand.

$$dT/de = \bar{\dot{D}}_e + \dot{\dot{S}}_e - (G\dot{\hat{C}}_b/q)$$

$$= \text{(direct effects)} + \text{(spillover effects with } dB^g = dq = 0)$$

$$+ \text{(spillover effect due to the change in } B^g). \quad (3.16)$$

Thus, in this case, the likelihood that a devaluation improves the balance of trade is increased.

A devaluation financed with a change in the bond price (i.e., $G\,de = (B^g - B_o^g)\,dq > 0$ and $dG = dM^g = dq = 0$) has an ambiguous effect on the balance of trade. In addition to the direct and spillover effects of a money-financed devaluation, there is the direct effect of the change in the bond price on consumption demand and current supply of goods and the spillover effects of the change in the bond price on consumption demand (via its effect on the bond ration). An increase in the bond price (when $B^g - B_o^g > 0$) leads to a substitution of goods for bonds by the household ($\hat{C}_q > 0$) and a substitution of planned production for bonds by the firm ($\hat{B}_q^* < 0$, I_q^*, $E_q^* > 0$, and $Y_q^* < 0$). So the direct effect of an increase in the bond price complements the spillover effects of the devaluation. The sign of the spillover effects of a change in the bond price on consumption demand is ambiguous because, as the bond price increases, the firm reduces its demand for bonds and increases its demand for labor (substitution effect). The increase in the demand for labor leads to an increase in consumption demand (wealth effect), whereas the decrease in the supply of loanable funds reduces the household's disposable wealth, which reduces consumption demand. Therefore, the net effect of spillovers due to an increase in the bond price on consumption demand is ambiguous. If a reduction in the bond price is called for (when $B^g - B_o^g < 0$), a sufficient condition for an improvement in the balance of trade is that the direct effects dominate the spillover effects.

$$dT/de = \bar{\dot{D}}_e + \dot{\dot{S}}_e + (\dot{\hat{C}}_q - Y_q^*)[G/(B^g \overset{?}{-} B_o^g)]$$

$$+ (\dot{\hat{C}}_b \bar{B}_q^* + \dot{\hat{C}}_n \dot{E}_q^*)[G/(B^g \overset{?}{-} B_o^g)]$$

$$= \text{(direct effects of devaluation)}$$

$$+ \text{(spillover effects of devaluation)}$$

$$+ \text{(direct effect of a change in bond price)}$$

$$+ \text{(spillover effects of a change in bond price)}.$$
$$(3.17)$$

If the direct effect of the decrease in the bond price dominates its spillover effects, then the likelihood of an improvement in the balance of trade is greater than under the case of money-financed devaluation.

3.4 The real wage, employment, and the balance of trade

A reduction in the nominal wage (with a constant e) leads to higher employment ($E_w^* < 0$) as the firm substitutes the relatively cheap labor input for goods input ($I_w^* > 0$).

The decrease in the nominal wage affects the balance of trade through three channels: (1) the reduction in the demand for goods as input, which increases the current supply of goods ($Y^* = Y_o^* - I^*$); (2) the change in the household's labor income, which affects its demand for goods ($\hat{C}_n E_w^* + \hat{C}_w$); and (3) the spillover effect of the change in the household's bond ration ($B_w^* > 0$) on its demand for goods ($\hat{C}_b > 0$). The spillover effect from the bond market complements the direct effects of devaluation on the balance of trade; this is because a reduction in the nominal wage leads to lower demand for bonds on the part of the firm, which reduces the household's bond ration and causes a decrease in consumption demand (disposable wealth is reduced). On the other hand, the spillover effect from the labor market increases consumption demand as the firm substitutes the relatively cheap labor input for goods input. Thus, the net effect on the balance of trade is ambiguous.

$$dT/dw = (\overset{+}{\hat{C}_w} - \overset{-}{Y_w^*}) + (\overset{+}{\hat{C}_b}\overset{+}{B_w^*} + \overset{+}{\hat{C}_n}\overset{-}{E_w^*})$$

$$= \text{(direct effects)} + \text{(spillover effects)} \qquad (3.18)$$

If the direct effect of the change in the nominal wage on consumption demand and the supply of goods plus the spillover effect from the bond market exceeds the spillover effect from the labor market, then the balance of trade unambiguously improves with a decrease in the nominal wage ($dT/dw > 0$).

CHAPTER 4

Households and firms rationed in the credit market

This chapter examines domestic-policy effectiveness in a small, open economy in a short-run equilibrium characterized by unemployment and general excess demand for loanable funds. In this environment, households are rationed as sellers in the labor and bond markets, and firms are rationed as sellers of bonds. Thus, the model considered here is a hybrid of those in Chapters 2 and 3. An interesting feature of this model is that it permits treating credit rationing as a policy instrument; that is, we can examine, in addition to the effects of the macroeconomic policies previously considered, the effects on unemployment and the balance of trade of a reallocation of the existing stock of loanable funds among firms and households. After a brief specification of the behavioral assumptions, the comparative static properties of the model are examined.

4.1 The model

The small, open economy is populated by a representative household, a representative firm, the treasury, and the central bank. Purchasing-power parity and a rigid world price of goods, normalized to one, imply that the exchange rate e is the domestic price level. This exchange rate is maintained by the central bank. The nominal wage w and the nominal bond price q are also rigid in the short run. There is no capital mobility.

The government's nominal purchase of goods eG, the change in the stock of domestic money $(M^g - M_0^g)$, and the change in the value of interest bearing public debt $(qB^g - qB_0^g)$ are related through the treasury's budget constraint as follows:

$$eG = M^g - M_0^g + (qB^g - qB_0^g) - B_0^g, \qquad (4.1)$$

where B_0^g is the interest payment on outstanding debt. The level of aggregation of this model (i.e., one firm and one household) for the regime under consideration, with excess supply of bonds by the firm and the household and a positive aggregate bond ration, requires that the treasury be a net buyer of bonds (i.e., $b^g = B_0^g - B^g > 0$, where b^g is the treasury's net purchases of bonds). In addition to choosing its purchases of goods and the method of financing them, the government can alter by decree the nominal wage w, the exchange rate e, the nominal bond price q, and the allocation of bonds between the household and the firm. The firm's bond ration is $b^* = fb^g$, where f is the firm's share of net purchases of bonds by the domestic government. It follows, therefore, that the household's bond ration is $b = (1 - f)b^g$.

The representative firm is rationed as a seller in the bond market; so it has effective demands for the labor input $\tilde{E}^*(e, w, q, b^*)$, the goods input $\tilde{I}^*(e, w, q, b^*)$, money $\tilde{M}^*(e, w, q, b^*)$, and bonds $\tilde{B}^* = B_0^* - b^*$. There is a one-period lag in production so that the stock of domestically produced goods Y_0^* is fixed in the short run. Thus, the current supply of goods is $\tilde{Y}^* = Y_0^* - \tilde{I}^*$.

The representative household is rationed as a seller in the labor and bond markets. It has effective demands for goods $\hat{C}(e, w, q, n, b)$, money $\hat{M}(e, w, q, n, b)$, leisure $\hat{H} = Z - n$, and bonds $\hat{B} = B_0 - b$, where Z is total time, n the labor ration, and b the household's bond ration (as defined above).

4.2   Comparative statics

The domestic economy is in a temporary equilibrium with rationing when the behavior of all agents is mutually consistent. In particular, the equilibrium of this regime requires that the domestic firm, based on its bond ration, regenerate the household's labor ration. This equilibrium is characterized by

$$\hat{L} = \tilde{E}^*(\dot{e}, \bar{w}, \dot{q}, \dot{b}^*) = n \tag{4.2}$$

and

$$b^g = b^* + b. \tag{4.3}$$

The balance of trade in real units is

$$T = \hat{C}(\bar{e}, \dot{w}, \dot{q}, \dot{n}, \dot{b}) + G - \tilde{Y}^*(\dot{e}, \bar{w}, \dot{q}, \bar{b}^*). \tag{4.4}$$

Replacing $B^g - B_0^g$ with $-b^g$ in the treasury's budget constraint yields

$$eG = M^g - M_0^g - qb^g - B_0^g. \tag{4.5}$$

Substituting $fb^g = b^*$ and $(1 - f)b^g = b$ into (4.2) and (4.4) yields

$$\hat{L} = \tilde{E}^*(e, w, q, fb^g) = n, \tag{4.6}$$

and

$$T = \hat{C}(e, w, q, n, (1 - f)b^g) + G - \tilde{Y}^*(e, w, q, fb^g). \tag{4.7}$$

Total differentiation of (4.5), (4.6), and (4.7) yields the following system of equations:

$$
\begin{bmatrix}
1 & -\hat{C}_n & (f\tilde{Y}^*_{b^*} - (1-f)\hat{C}_b) \\
0 & 1 & -f\tilde{E}^*_{b^*} \\
0 & 0 & -q
\end{bmatrix}
\begin{bmatrix}
dT \\
dn \\
db^g
\end{bmatrix}
=
$$
$$
\begin{bmatrix}
(\hat{C}_e - \tilde{Y}^*_e)\,de + (\hat{C}_w - \tilde{Y}^*_w)\,dw + (\hat{C}_q - \tilde{Y}^*_q)\,dq + (-\tilde{Y}^*_{b^*} - \hat{C}_b)\,b^g df + dG \\
\tilde{E}^*_e\,de + \tilde{E}^*_w\,dw + \tilde{E}^*_q\,dq + \tilde{E}^*_{b^*}\,b^g\,df \\
e\,dG + G\,de - dM^g + b^g\,dq
\end{bmatrix}.
$$

$$(4.8)$$

4.3   Monetary and fiscal policies, employment, and the balance of trade

An expansionary monetary policy (i.e., $dM^g = -q\,dB^g > 0$ and $dG = de = dq = 0$) reduces the supply of bonds and thus enables the household and the firm to increase their liquidity (i.e., supply more bonds). The firm will use some of the borrowed funds to increase its purchases of factor inputs. This increases the demand for labor and decreases the current supply of goods. The increase in the demand for labor and the increase in liquidity of the household leads to an increase in consumption demand. The higher consumption demand and the lower supply of goods leads to a deterioration of the balance of trade.

$$dn/dM^g = f(1/q)\overset{+}{\tilde{E}^*_{b^*}} > 0, \tag{4.9}$$

$$dT/dM^g = (1-f)(1/q)\overset{+}{\tilde{C}_b} - f(1/q)(\overset{-}{\tilde{Y}^*_{b^*}} + \overset{+}{\hat{C}_n}\overset{+}{\tilde{E}^*_{b^*}}) > 0. \tag{4.10}$$

A bond-financed increase in government spending (i.e., $e\,dG = q\,dB^g > 0$ and $dM^g = dq = de = 0$) crowds out the household and the firm from the bond market. The firm will lower its planned production and thus will need fewer inputs. The lower demand for goods input increases the current supply for goods, and lower employment reduces consumption demand. In addition, there is the direct effect of an increase in government purchases on aggregate demand and its indirect effect via the bond ration on consumption demand. The former increases aggregate demand, and the latter reduces it. However, the net effect is a deterioration of the balance of trade.

$$dn/dG = -(e/q)f\overset{+}{\tilde{E}^*_{b^*}} < 0, \tag{4.11}$$

$$dT/dG = 1 - (e/q)[(1-f)\overset{+}{\hat{C}_b} - f\overset{-}{\tilde{Y}^*_{b^*}}] - f(e/q)\overset{+}{\hat{C}_n}\overset{+}{\tilde{E}^*_{b^*}}$$
$$= f(1/q)(\overset{+}{\tilde{M}^*_{b^*}} + \overset{+}{\tilde{M}_n}\overset{+}{\tilde{E}^*_{b^*}}) + (1-f)(1/q)\overset{+}{\tilde{M}_b} > 0, \tag{4.12}$$

where we have substituted for $\hat{C}_b$, $\tilde{Y}_{b*}^*$, and $\hat{C}_n\tilde{E}_{b*}^*$ from the household's and the firm's budget constraints.[1]

4.4 Devaluation, employment, and the balance of trade

Case 1: Money-financed devaluation

A money-financed devaluation of the domestic currency (i.e., $G\,de = dM^g > 0$ and $dG = dB^g = dq = 0$) leaves the stock of bonds unchanged. Thus, the household's and the firm's credit rations are unchanged. The higher price of goods induces the firm to substitute the relatively cheaper labor input for goods input. The increase in the demand for labor leads to an increase in consumption demand (wealth effect), whereas the reduced demand for goods as input leads to an increase in the current supply of goods. The former worsens the balance of trade, but the latter improves it. In addition, there is substitution of money for goods by the household, which improves the balance of trade. Therefore, the net effect on the balance of trade is ambiguous.

$$dT/de = \overset{-}{D_e} + \overset{+}{S_e}$$
$$= \text{(direct effects)} + \text{(spillover effect)}, \qquad (4.13)$$

where $D_e = (\overset{-}{\hat{C}_e} - \overset{+}{\tilde{Y}_e^*})$, and $S_e = \overset{+}{\hat{C}_n}\overset{+}{\tilde{E}_e^*}$.

If the direct effect exceeds the spillover effects, the balance of trade improves as a result of the devaluation.

Case 2: Devaluation accompanied by a reduction in G

The effect of a devaluation of the domestic currency accompanied by a reduction in government spending (i.e., $G\,de = -e\,dG > 0$ and $dB^g = dM^g = dq = 0$) on employment is identical to that of money-financed devaluation because in both cases the stock of bonds is unchanged. However, because the reduction in government spending improves the balance of trade directly, the likelihood of an improvement in the balance of trade is greater in this case than in the case of money-financed devaluation.

$$dT/de = [\overset{-}{D_e} - (G/e)] + \overset{+}{S_e}$$
$$= \text{(direct effects)} + \text{(spillover effect)}. \qquad (4.14)$$

Case 3: Bond-financed devaluation

If a devaluation is accompanied by an increase in the stock of bonds (i.e., $G\,de = q\,dB^g > 0$ and $dG = dM^g = dq = 0$), there will be direct

---

[1] See Section 2.6 for a similar proof.

and spillover effects of the change in the stock of bonds in addition to the direct and spillover effects of the change in the exchange rate. As the stock of bonds increases, the household and the firm find their disposable wealth reduced. In response to this, the firm decreases its planned production, and the household decreases its purchases of goods. The decrease in planned production leads to a decrease in the demand for inputs, which increases the current supply of goods. The decrease in employment further decreases the household's demand for goods (wealth effect). Therefore, the increase in the stock of bonds increases the likelihood of an improvement in the balance of trade as a result of the devaluation. However, only when the direct effect of the exchange rate on employment (substitution effect) exceeds the direct effect of the increase in the supply of bonds on employment (wealth effect) can we be sure that the devaluation will lead to an increase in employment.

$$dn/de = \overset{+}{\underset{-}{\bar{E}}}{}^*_e - f(G/q)\overset{+}{\underset{-}{\bar{E}}}{}^*_{b*}$$

$\quad$ = (direct effect of devaluation)

$\quad\quad$ + (direct effect of the increase in B^g). $\qquad$ (4.15)

$$dT/de = \bar{D}_e + \overset{+}{S}_e - f(G/q)\overset{+}{\underset{-}{\hat{C}}}{}_n\overset{+}{\underset{-}{\bar{E}}}{}^*_{b*} - (\overset{+}{G}/q)[-\bar{Y}^*_{b*}f + (1-f)\overset{+}{\underset{-}{\hat{C}}}{}_b]$$

$\quad$ = (direct effect of devaluation)

$\quad\quad$ + (spillover effect of devaluation)

$\quad\quad$ + (spillover effect of the increase in B^g)

$\quad\quad$ + (direct effect of the increase in B^g).

$\qquad\qquad\qquad\qquad\qquad\qquad\qquad\qquad\qquad\qquad$ (4.16)

Case 4: Devaluation and a reduction in the bond price

In this regime, the government is a net buyer of bonds (i.e., $B^g - B^g_o < 0$). Thus, a devaluation may be accompanied by a reduction in the bond price (i.e., $G\,de = (B^g - B^g_o)\,dq > 0$ and $dB^g = dM^g = dG = 0$). The decrease in the bond price reduces the disposable wealth of both the firm and the household. In response to this, the household reduces its demand for goods, and the firm reduces its planned production. With a lower planned production, the demand for inputs is reduced; thus, employment decreases, and the current supply of goods increases. The decrease in the level of employment further reduces the demand for goods. Therefore, the decrease in the bond price increases the likelihood that a devaluation will improve the balance of trade. However, as in the case of a bond-financed devaluation, the net effect on employment is uncertain. Only when the effect of the devaluation on labor demand exceeds the effect of the reduction in the bond price on labor demand will there be increased employment.

$$dn/de = \overset{\pm}{\bar{E}}{}^*_e + \overset{\pm}{\bar{E}}{}^*_q[G/(B^g - B^g_o)]$$
$$= \text{(effect of the devaluation)}$$
$$+ \text{(effect of the decrease in the bond price)}. \tag{4.17}$$

$$dT/de = \bar{D}_e + \overset{+}{S}_e + (\overset{\pm}{\bar{C}}_q - \overset{-}{\tilde{Y}}{}^*_q)[G/(B^g - B^g_o)] + \overset{+}{\hat{C}}_n\overset{\pm}{\bar{E}}{}^*_q[G/(B^g - B^g_o)]$$
$$= \text{(direct effect of devaluation)}$$
$$+ \text{(spillover effect of devaluation)}$$
$$+ \text{(direct effect of the decrease in the bond price)}$$
$$+ \text{(spillover effect of the decrease in the bond price)}.$$
$$\tag{4.18}$$

4.5   Reallocation of the stock of loanable funds

Because there is a general excess demand for loanable funds in this regime, it is interesting to examine the impact on employment and the balance of trade of a reallocation of the stock of loanable funds between the firm and the household.

An increase in f reduces the disposable wealth of the household and increases the disposable wealth of the firm. In response to this, the firm will increase its demand for inputs (wealth effect). The increase in the demand for goods used as input reduces the current supply of goods, which worsens the balance of trade. The increase in demand for labor increases consumption demand (wealth effect), while the household's lower disposable wealth reduces it. Thus, the net effect on the balance of trade is ambiguous.[2]

$$dn/df = b^g\overset{\pm}{\tilde{E}}{}^*_{b*} > 0 \tag{4.19}$$

$$dT/df = b^g(-\overset{-}{\tilde{Y}}{}^*_{b*} - \overset{\pm}{\hat{C}}_b) + b^g\overset{+}{\hat{C}}_n\overset{\pm}{\bar{E}}{}^*_{b*}$$
$$= \text{(direct effect)} + \text{(spillover effect)}. \tag{4.20}$$

If the direct effect of the reallocation of the stock of loanable funds on the current supply of goods plus the spillover effect on consumption

---

[2] If the existing allocation of credit is a function of the riskiness of the debtors, then the government can bring about a reallocation of the existing stock of credit by affecting the risk of loans to the firm. This can be done by insuring the loans to the firm.

demand is greater (less) than the direct effect of the reallocation on consumption demand, the balance of trade deteriorates (improves) as a result of an increase in the firm's share of the existing stock of loanable funds.

4.6   The real wage, employment, and the balance of trade

In this regime, the firm has an effective demand for labor that reflects its bond ration, whereas the household has an effective demand for goods that is conditional on its bond and labor rations; the bond rations are independent of prices. In this environment, a decrease in the nominal wage (with a fixed exchange rate) leads to an increase in demand for labor as the firm substitutes the relatively cheap labor input for the goods input. As the demand for goods used as input decreases, the current supply of goods increases, which improves the balance of trade. The increase in employment leads to an increase in the demand for goods by the household, while the decrease in the nominal wage reduces it. Thus, the net effect on consumption demand and the balance of trade is uncertain.

$$dT/dw = (\overset{+}{\hat{C}}_w - \bar{Y}^*_w) + \overset{+}{\hat{C}}_n\bar{E}^*_w$$

$$= \text{(direct effects)} + \text{(spillover effects)}. \tag{4.21}$$

If the direct effects exceed the spillover effect, the balance of trade will improve with a reduction of the nominal wage.

CHAPTER 5

Central-bank portfolio selection and stabilization policies

In macroeconomic models, the behavior of the government is often exogenous, except for its budget constraint, which relates the stock of assets (money and bonds) and net government revenue (taxes minus transfers and interest payments on national debt) to the level of government spending. In such formulations the government is a consolidation of the treasury and the central bank, and open-market operations are entirely exogenous.

This level of aggregation and exogenous specification of government behavior omits some of the determinants of the short-run values of crucial macroeconomic variables, such as asset prices (e.g., exchange rates and interest rates).

In this chapter, as a first step toward overcoming these shortcomings, the government is disaggregated into the treasury and the central bank. The behavior of the treasury is exogenous, as mentioned.[1] In contrast, the behavior of the central bank is endogenous, the outcome of portfolio optimization subject to endowments and stabilization constraints.

The implications of portfolio optimization by the central bank are examined for the efficacy of the treasury's policies in the short run. It is demonstrated that the impact of monetary and fiscal policies on the exchange rate, interest rate, and employment are conditional on the characterization of the short-run equilibrium in which the economy finds itself. The fact that the effects on employment are conditional on the initial equilibrium is already known from antecedent, related models.[2] What is new here is the disaggregation of the government into the treasury and the central bank and the specification of the behavior of the central bank. A result of these extensions is that the impact of the treasury's policies on asset prices is conditional on the initial equilibrium.

It is assumed that the central bank has two functions: stabilization and portfolio selection. The stabilization function is exogenously specified in terms of the primary policy objectives of the central bank, in particular,

---

[1] In practice, there are substantial lags in implementing a change in government spending. For this reason we treat the behavior of the treasury as exogenous in the short run.

[2] See Chapter 1 for the context of this book.

exchange-rate and interest-rate targets. The portfolio-selection behavior is influenced by current and anticipated stabilization demands for assets (transactions demand) and by the anticipated rate of return on assets (speculative demand). The stabilization function imposes constraints, in addition to the initial endowments, on the central bank's portfolio selection. When stabilization constraints are not binding, the central bank's portfolio choice is constrained only by its initial endowments. In this case, the central bank's demands are notional demands. However, when the central bank is committed to maintaining the current interest rate or the current exchange rate (the case of a binding stabilization constraint), then its demands for bonds or foreign currency may differ from its notional demands.

For example, consider the situation in which at the current exchange rate the central bank has an excess demand for foreign currency and an excess supply of domestic currency and domestic bonds. In this situation, if there are no primary targets to prevent the central bank from expressing its notional demands on asset markets, then the exchange rate and the interest rate will be affected by the central bank's purchase of foreign currency and sale of domestic bonds. However, the central bank may be prevented from expressing its notional demands for assets on the market because of its primary policy targets. In this example, if the central bank is committed to maintaining the current interest rate, then its demands for assets reflect this additional constraint. In effect, when a stabilization constraint is binding, a quantity ration is imposed on the central bank (in our example the central bank's stock of bonds will be determined by market conditions), which will cause it to revise its demands for non-rationed assets (domestic currency and foreign currency in our example). In this case, the central bank's demands will be effective demands. Because effective demands for non-rationed assets are functions of the quantity ration (as well as prices, expectations, and initial endowments), a change in the quantity ration will have spillover effects on markets for non-rationed assets. One contribution of this chapter is the demonstration that these spillover effects can alter domestic-policy effectiveness in a qualitative sense. Another contribution is that a theory of asset-market intervention is specified. A distinguishing feature of this theory is that asset-market intervention (e.g., managed float) emerges as the result of the central bank's portfolio selection subject to its stabilization policies and initial endowments.

5.1   Connections with earlier chapters

In earlier chapters, the effectiveness of macroeconomic policies were explored in regimes with private-sector rationing in asset markets; in particular, the household and/or the firm were rationed in the credit market. In this chapter, the focus of the analysis is on public-sector rationing in the asset markets. Private-sector rationing is imposed by the market. Public-sector rationing is self-imposed in the sense that it is the consequence of the conflict between the central bank's portfolio selection and its stabilization policies.

The model here differs from that used in earlier chapters in several respects. To focus the analysis on the implications of public-sector rationing in the asset markets, it is assumed that the interest rate is potentially flexible and that the household and the firm are not rationed in the credit market. The menu of assets is enlarged to include foreign assets. However, the assumption of no capital mobility is retained. The behavior of the foreign central bank is specified, which makes the supply of foreign assets to the domestic country endogenous. The exchange rate is potentially flexible and is determined by the interaction between the domestic and foreign central banks. The domestic government is dis-aggregated into treasury and central bank. However, the small-country assumption is retained.

5.2   The model

The setting is a small, open economy that is in a regime characterized by unemployment and a balance-of-trade deficit. The economy, being small, is not rationed in world markets for its produced goods. In this regime are subregimes that are distinguished by the nature of rationing in asset markets: for example, excess demand for foreign currency and excess supply of domestic bonds.

The economy produces a composite commodity by employing domestic labor and previously produced goods as input. The domestic economic agents are separated into four groups: a representative firm, a representative household, the treasury, and the central bank. There are five goods: labor services, produced goods, domestic currency, domestic bonds, and foreign currency (money and bonds aggregated).

The domestic firm holds only domestic assets and is a net seller in world product markets. The domestic household is a buyer in product markets and a seller in the domestic labor market, and it holds domestic assets. The domestic treasury is a buyer in product markets and the issuer of domestic assets. The domestic central bank holds a diversified portfolio of domestic and foreign assets.

The exchange rate e and the bond price q are potentially flexible, whereas in the short run the domestic nominal wage w and the world price level p^* are fixed. Purchasing-power parity (arbitrage in product markets) implies that the domestic price p is determined by the world price level and the exchange rate (i.e., $p = ep^*$). Normalization of world price level yields $p = e$.

Given a money wage that is rigid in the short run, there may be rationing in the labor market. For the regimes under consideration, there is unemployment. The household revises its demand for consumption goods and savings, taking the labor ration into account.

The domestic household and firm are not rationed in asset markets. They do not hold foreign currency, and so there are no private-capital movements. However, the interaction between domestic and foreign households and firms in international trade implies a net transactions demand for foreign currency. Central banks are the only direct participants in the foreign-exchange market. The transactions demand for foreign currency is a claim against the central bank of the deficit country. The settlement of international indebtedness may lead to foreign-exchange market intervention.

Central banks are assumed to be portfolio optimizers. To the extent that portfolio optimization is not inconsistent with their primary objectives (e.g., interest-rate target, exchange-rate target, and so forth), it determines the central banks's actions (intervention) in asset markets. If there is a conflict between a primary objective and portfolio selection, there may be rationing in the asset markets. The central bank will then revise its demands for unrationed assets. Through this channel, rationing in an asset market has general equilibrium spillover effects for other markets in the economy.

The behavior of the treasury and the central bank are elaborated in the following sections. Details of the behavior of the firm and the household were presented in Chapter 2, Sections 2.3 and 2.4.

5.3   The treasury

The treasury's purchases of goods G can be financed by issuing domestic currency ($M^g - M_o^g$) or domestic bonds ($B^g - B_o^g$) or by taxation. A treasury bond is a perpetuity that pays one unit of domestic currency per period (i.e., the intitial stock of bonds B_o^g is also the interest payment on outstanding debt). Taxes and transfers are assumed to be equal. The treasury's budget constraint is

$$eG = M^g - M_o^g + qB^g - (q + 1)B_o^g. \tag{5.1}$$

5.4   The central bank

The central bank has two functions: stabilization and portfolio selection. The stabilization function is exogenously specified in terms of the primary policy objectives of the central bank, which are

Exchange-rate target: $e(\min) \leqq e \leqq e(\max)$,

Interest-rate target: $q(\min) \leqq q \leqq q(\max)$.   (5.2)

These primary targets impose constraints (in addition to initial endowments) on the central bank's portfolio selection.[3]

The portfolio-selection behavior is influenced by current and anticipated stabilization demand for assets (transactions demand) and the anticipated rate of return on assets (speculative demand). If stabilization constraints are not binding, the central bank's portfolio choice will be notional. When a stabilization constraint is binding, a quantity ration is effectively imposed on the central bank that causes it to revise its demands; that is, the central bank's demands will be effective demands. The excess notional demand for (supply of) an asset persists because it is not expressed on the market. It is in this sense that the temporary equilibrium in asset markets will be characterized by rationing.

Before specifying the optimization problem of the central bank, some remarks about the source of demand for foreign currency are in order.

The sources of demand for foreign currency by the central bank are transactions demand and speculative demand. The transactions demand for foreign currency is a derived demand. Firms and households in each country hold only the currency of their country of residence, but the settlement of international transactions implies a net demand for foreign currency by the central bank. The central bank's speculative demand for foreign currency is due to uncertainty about the future economic environment. The central bank is assumed to be risk averse and thus will choose a diversified portfolio of assets.

If, as assumed, the domestic country has a balance-of-trade deficit, then the central bank's holdings of domestic money increase as domestic households try to acquire the necessary foreign exchange to engage in trade with foreign firms. The increase is given by

$$eT \quad \text{for } T > 0,$$ (5.3)

where T is the balance of trade in real units (i.e., $T = \tilde{C} + G - Y^*$). Correspondingly, the domestic central bank's stock of foreign money is reduced by T (for $T > 0$).

Once the domestic households have acquired the foreign exchange, these funds are distributed to foreign firms in return for goods. Thus, at the initial exchange rate, the composition of the portfolio of the surplus

---

[3] A money-supply target could be specified as follows:

$$M(\min) \leqslant M^s \leqslant M(\max),$$

where $M(\min)$ ($M(\max)$) is the lower (upper) limit on the money supply M^s.

country's central bank is not affected by a change in the balance of trade. However, if the deficit country's central bank attempts to restore to some degree its stock of foreign-currency reserves, it must bid up the exchange rate. Because the foreign central bank's demands for assets are functions of prices (as we shall see), the composition of the portfolio of the surplus country's central bank will be affected by a change in the balance of trade.

The optimization problem of the domestic central bank when the domestic country has a balance-of-trade deficit is given by the following:

Maximize $V^d(M^d, B^d, m^d)$

Subject to $M^d + qB^d + em^d = (M_o^d + eT) + (q + 1)B_o^d + e(m_o^d - T),$

$e(\text{min}) \leqq e \leqq e(\text{max}),$

and $q(min) \leqq q \leqq q(\text{max}),$ (5.4)

where $V^d(\ )$ is a derived utility function that is strictly quasi-concave in domestic currency M^d, domestic bonds B^d, and foreign currency m^d, and where M_o^d, B_o^d, and m_o^d are initial endowments of assets.[4]

The solution to the optimization problem of the central bank when the primary policy objectives are not binding will be called the *notional solution*. The notional demands are

$M^d(e, q),$

$B^d(e, q),$

and $m^d(e, q).$ (5.5)

The portfolio of the domestic central bank is influenced by its expectations about the future economic environment. For example, because the balance-of-trade deficit reduces the foreign-currency reserves of the deficit country, it follows that the expectations of the future balance of trade shoud play an important role in the portfolio-selection behavior of the central bank. In this model, the effect of the expected future balance of trade and all other variables that are subject to uncertainty is imbedded in the elasticities of the demand functions. It is assumed that the central banks view all assets as normal and gross substitutes (which admittedly sidesteps the important question of signing the elasticities of the demand functions). It follows that

$$M_e^d, B_e^d > 0, \quad m_e^d < 0, \quad M_q^d, m_q^d > 0 \quad \text{and} \quad B_q^d < 0. \quad (5.6)$$

---

[4] This is a prototype model with no commercial banks. For this reason the central bank's portfolio choice is conditional on its initial endowment of domestic money. However, it will be clear that the main conclusions of this chapter are not affected by this formulation.

When the central bank's portfolio selection is restricted by its primary policy objectives, there will be an excess notional demand or supply of assets at equilibrium that persists because it is not expressed on the market.

If the $e(\max)$ or $e(\min)$ constraint is binding, then the domestic central bank is rationed in the foreign-exchange market. The domestic central bank's foreign-exchange ration is $m = m_o^f + m_o^d - m^f - T$, where from here on superscript f denotes the foreign central bank's asset holdings. The rationed domestic central bank will revise its demands for other assets to reflect its foreign-exchange ration m. In this case, the effective demands are

$$\tilde{M}^d(\underline{e}, q, m),$$
$$\tilde{B}^d(\underline{e}, q, m),$$
and $\quad \tilde{m}^d = m, \qquad\qquad\qquad\qquad\qquad\qquad (5.7)$

where $\underline{e} \ \varepsilon \ [e(\min), e(\max)]$ is the exchange rate maintained by central bank's intervention in the foreign-exchange market.

It is assumed that

$$\tilde{B}_m^d, \tilde{B}_q^d, \tilde{M}_m^d < 0 \quad \text{and} \quad \tilde{M}_q^d > 0. \qquad\qquad\qquad (5.8)$$

If the $q(\max)$ or $q(\min)$ constraint is binding, then the domestic central bank will be rationed in the domestic bond market. The central bank's bond ration is $b = B^g - B^z$, where B^z is the aggregate demand for bonds on the part of domestic households, domestic firms, and the foreign central bank. In this case, the effective demands are

$$\hat{M}^d(e, q, b),$$
$$\hat{m}^d(e, q, b),$$
and $\quad \hat{B}^d = b, \qquad\qquad\qquad\qquad\qquad\qquad (5.9)$

where $\underline{q} \ \varepsilon \ [q(\min), q(\max)]$ is the domestic nominal price of treasury bonds, which is maintained by the central bank's intervention in the bond market. It is assumed that

$$\hat{m}_e^d, \hat{M}_b^d, \hat{m}_b^d < 0 \quad \text{and} \quad \hat{M}_e^d > 0. \qquad\qquad\qquad (5.10)$$

The foreign central bank is assumed to choose an optimal portfolio of M^f, B^f, and m^f. The optimization problem of the foreign central bank is similar to that of the domestic central bank except that, for the regimes that we shall consider, it is assumed that the foreign central bank is not rationed in the asset markets. The notional-demand functions of the foreign central bank are

$$M^f(e, q),$$
$$B^f(e, q),$$
and $m^f(e, q).$ (5.11)

It is assumed that the foreign central bank views all assets as normal and gross substitutes so that

$$M_e^f, M_q^f, B_e^f, m_q^f > 0 \quad \text{and} \quad B_q^f, m_e^f < 0.$$ (5.12)

5.5   Comparative statics

In this section the objective is to demonstrate the implications of the central bank's portfolio-selection and stabilization policies for the efficacy of the treasury's policies in short-run equilibria with rationing. To do this, several economic environments are considered that are distinguished by the type of rationing in asset markets. Throughout the analysis, the domestic country is assumed to be in a state of unemployment and trade deficit and not rationed in the product market. Also, the domestic household and the domestic firm are assumed to face no quantity constraints on their purchases or sales of assets.

In this economic environment, the domestic firm is not rationed. Its notional demands for labor, domestic currency, and domestic bonds are $E^*(e, q)$, $M^*(e, q)$, and $B^*(e, q)$, where here and henceforth we suppress the dependence of the demand functions of the firm and the household on the nominal wage. This is justified because the nominal wage is assumed to be rigid in the short run. The firm's notional current supply of goods is $Y^*(e, q)$. The household is rationed in the labor market. Its effective demands for goods and assets are $\tilde{C}(e, q, n)$, $\tilde{M}(e, q, n)$, and $\tilde{B}(e, q, n)$. The household's effective supply of labor is $\tilde{L} = n = E^*$. Substituting for n in the effective demands of the household yields

$$\tilde{C}(e, q, E^*(e, q)) = \ddot{C}(e, q),$$
$$\tilde{M}(e, q, E^*(e, q)) = \ddot{M}(e, q),$$
and $\tilde{B}(e, q, E^*(e, q)) = \ddot{B}(e, q).$

It is assumed that the direct effects of e and q on the household's demands dominate indirect effects via the labor market.[5] That is,

$$\ddot{M}_q, \ddot{C}_q, \ddot{M}_e, \ddot{B}_e > 0, \quad \ddot{C}_e < 0, \quad \text{and} \quad \ddot{B}_q < 0.$$ (5.13)

---

[5] This assumption is justified in this chapter because the focus of the analysis is on the interaction between the treasury and the central bank. However, in general, the spillover effects should be quantified for correct policy prescriptions.

The balance of trade for this regime is

$$T(\bar{e}, \dot{q}, \overset{+}{G}) = \ddot{C}(\bar{e}, \dot{q}) + G - Y^*(\dot{e}, \bar{q}). \tag{5.14}$$

The central banks may be rationed in the asset markets, and there are several cases to consider, depending on the characteristics of this rationing. The analysis begins with the case of no rationing in the asset markets.

Regime I: No rationing in asset markets

Under this regime the central banks have notional demands for assets. The notional-demand functions of the domestic central bank for domestic currency, domestic bonds, and foreign currency are $M^d(e, q)$, $B^d(e, q)$, and $m^d(e, q)$. The notional-demand functions of the foreign central bank are $M^f(e, q)$, $B^f(e, q)$, and $m^f(e, q)$. This domestic economy is in a temporary equilibrium with rationing when the decisions of all agents are mutually consistent. That is, the household's effective demands for goods, money, and bonds (conditional on the labor ration n), the central bank's notional demands for assets, and the firm's notional demands for goods and assets must lead to an exchange rate and a bond price that will induce the firm to demand n units of labor. The temporary equilibrium of this regime is described by the following:

Foreign-exchange market equilibrium:

$$m^f(\bar{e}, \dot{q}) - m^f_o + m^d(\bar{e}, \dot{q}) - m^d_o + T(\bar{e}, \dot{q}, \overset{+}{G}) = 0. \tag{5.15}$$

Bond-market equilibrium:

$$B^g = \ddot{B}(\dot{e}, \bar{q}) + B^*(\dot{e}, \bar{q}) + B^f(\dot{e}, \bar{q}) + B^d(\dot{e}, \bar{q}) = B^z(\dot{e}, \bar{q}), \tag{5.16}$$

where $B^g(B^z)$ is the aggregate supply of (demand for) bonds.

Domestic employment level:

$$n = E^*(\dot{e}, \dot{q}). \tag{5.17}$$

The domestic treasury's budget constraint is

$$eG = M^g - M^g_o + qB^g - (q + 1)B^g_o. \tag{5.18}$$

Substituting from the bond-market equilibrium condition for B^g into the treasury's budget constraint yields

$$eG = M^g - M^g_o + qB^z(\dot{e}, \bar{q}) - (q + 1)B^g_o. \tag{5.19}$$

Total differentiation of (5.15) and (5.19) gives the following system of equations:

$$\begin{bmatrix} -(m^f + m^d + T)_e & -(m^f + m^d + T)_q \\ (eG - qB)_e & (qB_o^g - qB^z)_q \end{bmatrix} \begin{bmatrix} de \\ dq \end{bmatrix} = \begin{bmatrix} dG \\ dM^g - edG \end{bmatrix},$$

(5.20)

where $(.)_x$ denotes the partial derivative of the variable in parentheses with respect to x. The determinant of the matrix of coefficients is positive because

$$(eG - qB^z)_e = (\ddot{M}(e, q) + M^*(e, q) + M^d(e, q) + M^f(e, q))_e$$
$$\equiv (M^z(e, q))_e > 0,$$

and $\quad (qB_o^g - qB^z)_q = (M^z - M_o^g - B_o^g - eG)_q$
$$= (em^f - em_o^f + em^d - em_o^d + e\ddot{C} - eY^* + M^z$$
$$- M_o^g - B_o^g)_q > 0.$$

(5.21)

Open-market operations: A reduction in the national debt (via an open-market operation by the treasury) leads to a lower interest rate as the bond price is bid up. This affects the demand for foreign currency through several channels. The lower interest rate leads to a higher transactions demand for foreign currency because consumption increases and current supply decreases. The higher transactions demand changes the composition of the portfolio of the domestic central bank at the initial exchange rate. This, in combination with portfolio substitution of domestic and foreign central banks due to the higher bond price, leads to a net excess demand for foreign exchange. The final result is a higher exchange rate and a higher bond price.

$$de/dM^g = \dot{A}(m^f + m^d + T)_q^+ > 0,$$

(5.22)

and $\quad dq/dM^g = -\dot{A}(m^f + m^d + T)_e^- > 0,$

(5.23)

where A is the inverse of the determinant of the matrix of coefficients, and superscript $+$ in $(.)_x^+$ is the sign of $(.)_x$.

The exchange-rate depreciation increases the demand for labor as the firm substitutes the relatively cheaper labor input for the goods input. The increase in the bond price leads to substitution of planned production and domestic currency for bonds, thus leading to a further increase in the demand for labor.

$$dE^*/dM^g = \dot{E}_e^*(de/dM^g) + \dot{E}_q^*(dq/dM^g) > 0.$$

(5.24)

Fiscal policy: A bond-financed increase in the treasury's purchases of goods leads to a higher interest rate as the government offers a lower bond price. The lower bond price affects the exchange rate via two channels. It leads to a lower transactions demand for foreign currency as consumption demand decreases (substitution of bonds for goods), and the current supply of goods increases (substitution of bonds for planned production). The lower bond price also induces substitution of bonds for currencies in portfolios (i.e., speculative demand for foreign currency is reduced). On the other hand, the increase in the treasury's purchases of goods increases the transactions demand for foreign currency directly. However, it will be shown that the net effect is an increase in the demand for foreign currency, which leads to exchange-rate depreciation. As the exchange rate depreciates, the demand for bonds increases (bonds, foreign currency, and goods are substitutes), reducing the decrease in the bond price.

$$de/dG = \overset{+}{A}(qB_0^g - qB^z)_q^+ - \overset{+}{A}(em^f + em^d + eT)_q^+, \qquad (5.25)$$

$$dq/dG = e\overset{+}{A}(m^f + m^d + T)_c^- - \overset{+}{A}(eG - qB^z)_c^+ < 0. \qquad (5.26)$$

The exchange rate depreciates if $(qB_0^g - qB^z)_q^+ - (em^f + em^d + eT)_q^+ > 0$. Substitution from the treasury's budget constraint and foreign-exchange-market equilibrium condition yields

$$(qB_0^g - qB^z)_q = (em^f + em^d + e\ddot{C} - eY^* + M^z)_q,$$

but

$$(em^f + em^d + e\ddot{C} - eY^* + M^z)_q - (em^f + em^d + eT)_q$$
$$= (M^z - eG)_q = (qB_0^g - qB^z)_q > 0. \qquad (5.27)$$

The exchange-rate depreciation leads to substitution of labor for the goods input, whereas the increase in the interest rate leads to substitution of bonds for planned production and domestic currency. The net effect on employment is uncertain.

$$dE^*/dG = \overset{+}{E_e^*}(de/dG) + \overset{+}{E_q^*}(dq/dG). \qquad (5.28)$$

Regime II: *Domestic central bank rationed in the foreign-exchange market [binding e(max) constraint]*

Under this regime, the foreign central bank has notional demands for assets, and the domestic central bank has effective demands for assets. The notional demands of the foreign central bank are $M^f(e, q)$, $B^f(e, q)$, and $m^f(e, q)$. The effective demands of the domestic central bank are $\tilde{M}^d(e, q, m)$, $\tilde{B}^d(e, q, m)$, and $\tilde{m}^d = m$, where m is the foreign-exchange ration; see (5.30). The domestic economy is in a temporary equilibrium with rationing when the interest rate, labor ration, and foreign-currency ration regenerate themselves. In this regime, the household takes prices and the labor ration as given and expresses its effective demands for goods and assets; the firm expresses its notional demands for assets and factors of production, based on price signals; the domestic central bank takes its foreign-currency ration and prices as given and expresses its effective demands for the non-rationed assets; and the foreign central bank expresses its notional demands for assets based on price signals. When the decisions of all agents are mutually consistent with each other (prices and quantity rations regenerate themselves), the economy is in a temporary equilibrium with rationing. The following equations characterize this equilibrium:

Domestic employment level:

$$n = E^*(\dot{e}, \dot{q}). \tag{5.29}$$

Foreign exchange market equilibrium:

$$\tilde{m}^d = m = m_o^f - m^f(\bar{e}, \dot{q}) + m_o^d - T(\bar{e}, \dot{q}, \overset{+}{G}). \tag{5.30}$$

Domestic bond market equilibrium:

$$B^g = \ddot{B}(\dot{e}, \bar{q}) + B^*(\dot{e}, \bar{q}) + B^f(\dot{e}, \bar{q}) + \tilde{B}^d(\dot{e}, \bar{q}, \dot{m})$$
$$\equiv \tilde{B}^z(\dot{e}, \bar{q}, \dot{m}). \tag{5.31}$$

Substituting from the bond-market equilibrium condition for B^g in the treasury's budget constraint yields

$$eG = M^g - M_o^g + q\tilde{B}^z - (q + 1)B_o^g. \tag{5.32}$$

Total differentiation of (5.30) and (5.32) gives the following system of equations:

$$\begin{bmatrix} 1 & (m^f + T)_q \\ -q\tilde{B}_m^d & (qB_o^g - q\tilde{B}^z)_q \end{bmatrix} \begin{bmatrix} dm \\ dq \end{bmatrix} = \begin{bmatrix} -dG \\ dM^g - edG \end{bmatrix}. \tag{5.33}$$

The determinant of the matrix of the coefficients is

$$X = (qB_o^g - q\tilde{B}^z)_q + (m^f + T)_q q\tilde{B}_m^d$$
$$= (m^f + T)_q \{(qB_o^g - q\tilde{B}^z)_q/(m^f + T)_q + q\tilde{B}_m^d\}. \tag{5.34}$$

Replacing $q\tilde{B}_m^d$ with $(q\tilde{B}^d/m)(m/\tilde{B}^d)\tilde{B}_m^d$ and multiplying through by (e/e) yields

$$X = e(m^f + T)_q(\alpha - \beta\eta), \tag{5.35}$$

where

$$\alpha \doteq (qB_o^g - q\tilde{B}^z)_q/(em^f + eT)_q,$$
$$\beta = (q\tilde{B}^d/em), \text{ and}$$
$$\eta = -(m/\tilde{B}^d)(\tilde{B}_m^d).$$

Substitution from the treasury's budget constraint for $(qB_o^g - q\tilde{B}^z)$ implies

$$(qB_o^g - q\tilde{B}^z)_q = (-eG + M^g - M_o^g)_q. \tag{5.36}$$

Substitution from the foreign-exchange-market equilibrium condition for eG and from the domestic-money-market equilibrium condition for M^g yields

$$(qB_o^g - q\tilde{B}^z)_q = (em - em_o^d + em^f - em_o^f + e\ddot{C} - eY^* + \tilde{M}^z$$
$$- M_o^g)_q > 0, \tag{5.37}$$

where $\tilde{M}^z \equiv \ddot{M}(e, q) + M^*(e, q) + M^f(e, q) + \tilde{M}^d(e, q, m)$. It follows that

$$\alpha = (qB^g - q\tilde{B}^z)_q/(em^f + eT)_q > 1. \tag{5.38}$$

Therefore, the sign of X depends on the elasticity of the effective demand for bonds with respect to the foreign-exchange ration η and the relative shares of domestic bonds and foreign currency β in the portfolio of the domestic central bank.

$$X \gtrless 0 \quad \text{as} \quad \beta\eta \lessgtr \alpha. \tag{5.39}$$

Open-market operations: If the central bank's demands are notional, then a reduction in a treasury's interest-bearing debt, achieved by purchasing domestic bonds with domestic currency, pushes down the interest rate as the bond price is bid up. The decline in the interest rate leads to the substitution of planned production for bonds, causing higher demand for labor and goods input. The increased demand for goods as input leads to a lower current supply of goods, which in combination with the increase in consumption (substitution effect) leads to a deterioration of the balance of trade.

However, when the domestic central bank is committed to maintaining the current exchange rate, its demands are effective demands. Thus, an increase in the transactions demand for foreign exchange will have spillover effects on the bond market because of the dependence of the central bank's effective-demand functions on the foreign-exchange ration. The net effect on the interest rate depends on the elasticity of the domestic bonds η and the relative shares of domestic bonds and foreign currency β in its portfolio.

The interest rate will decrease (increase) and the foreign-exchange ration will decrease (increase) if $\beta\eta$ is less than (greater than) α:

$$dm/dM^g = -X^{-1}(m^f + T)_q^+, \tag{5.40}$$

and

$$dq/dM^g = X^{-1},\qquad\qquad(5.41)$$

with sign (X) = sign $(\alpha - \beta\eta)$.

The decrease (increase) in the interest rate leads to the substitution of planned production for bonds (bonds for planned production) causing an increase (decrease) in both the demand for labor and the demand for goods as inputs.

Fiscal policy: A bond-financed increase in the treasury's purchases of goods leads to a change in the interest rate and the balance of trade. A change in the interest rate leads to portfolio substitution on the part of all asset holders. A change in the balance of trade affects the portfolio choice of the central banks because of its impact on the composition of the current portfolio and the foreign-exchange ration.

As in the case of open-market operations, the net effects on foreign-exchange ration and interest rate depend on the elasticity of the domestic central bank's effective-demand function for bonds and the relative share of domestic bonds and foreign currency in its portfolio.

$$dm/dG = (-\alpha + 1)(em^f + eT)_q X^{-1}\qquad\qquad(5.42)$$

and

$$dq/dG = (-e)(1 - \beta\eta)X^{-1},\qquad\qquad(5.43)$$

with sign (X) = sign $(\alpha - \beta\eta)$.

If $\beta\eta > \alpha$, then an increase in the treasury's purchases will lead to an increase in the interest rate, an increase in the domestic central bank's foreign-exchange reserves, and lower employment. If $\alpha > \beta\eta > 1$, then the interest rate and the domestic central bank's foreign-exchange reserves will decrease. The decline in the interest rate will lead to a higher demand for labor (substitution of planned production for bonds).

Regime III: *Domestic central bank rationed in the bond market*
        [binding q(min) constraint]

Under this regime, the foreign central bank is not rationed. Its notional demands are $M^f(e, q)$, $B^f(e, q)$, and $m^f(e, q)$. The domestic central bank is rationed in the bond market. Its effective demands for domestic currency, foreign currency, and domestic bonds are $\hat{M}^d(e, q, b)$, $\hat{m}^d(e, q, b)$, and $\hat{B}^d = b$, where b is the bond ration; see (5.46). A temporary equilibrium of this regime is reached when the firm, the household, and the central banks express market demands that reproduce the price and quantity signals on which they were based. This equilibrium is characterized by the following equations:

Domestic employment:

$$n = E^*(\dot{e}, \dot{q}). \tag{5.44}$$

Foreign-exchange-market equilibrium:

$$m^f(\bar{e}, \dot{q}) - m_o^f + \hat{m}^d(\bar{e}, \dot{q}, \bar{b}) - m_o^d + T(\bar{e}, \dot{q}, \dot{G}) = 0, \tag{5.45}$$

where T is the balance of trade.

Bond-market equilibrium:

$$b = B^g - \ddot{B}(\dot{e}, \dot{q}) - B^*(\dot{e}, \dot{q}) - B^f(\dot{e}, \dot{q}). \tag{5.46}$$

The domestic treasury's budget constraint is

$$eG = M^g - M_o^g + qB^g - (q + 1)B_o^g. \tag{5.47}$$

Solving for B^g in (5.46) and substituting into (5.47) yields

$$eG = M^g - M_o^g + qb + q\ddot{B}(e, q) + qB^*(e, q) + qB^f(e, q) \\ - (q + 1)B_o^g. \tag{5.48}$$

Total differentiation of (5.45) and (5.48) gives the following system of equations:

$$\begin{bmatrix} (m^f + \hat{m}^d + T)_e & \hat{m}_b^d \\ (eG - q\ddot{B} - qB^* - qB^f)_e & -q \end{bmatrix} \begin{bmatrix} de \\ db \end{bmatrix} = \begin{bmatrix} -dG \\ -edG + dM^g \end{bmatrix}. \tag{5.49}$$

The determinant of the matrix of coefficients is

$$\begin{aligned} \underline{X} &= (m^f + \hat{m}^d + T)_e(-q) - \hat{m}_b^d(eG - q\ddot{B} - qB^* - qB^f)_e \\ &= q(eG - q\ddot{B} - qB^* - qB^f)_e\{-(m^f + \hat{m}^d + T)_e/ \\ &\quad (eG - q\ddot{B} - qB^* - qB^f)_e - (\hat{m}_b^d/q)\}. \tag{5.50} \end{aligned}$$

Writing $\hat{m}_b^d$ as $(\hat{m}^d/b)(b/\hat{m}^d)\hat{m}_b^d$ and multiplying through by (e/e) yields

$$\underline{X} = (q/e)(eG - q\ddot{B} - qB^* - qB^f)_e(\alpha^* - \beta^*\eta^*), \tag{5.51}$$

where

$$\alpha^* \equiv -e(m^f + \hat{m}^d + T)_e/(eG - q\ddot{B} - qB^* - qB^f)_e,$$
$$\beta^* \equiv (e\hat{m}^d/qb), \text{ and}$$
$$\eta^* \equiv -(b/\hat{m}^d)(\hat{m}_b^d) > 0.$$

It is assumed that $(eG - q\ddot{B} - qB^* - qB^f)_e > 0$. This assumption is consistent with the results under regime I, where $(eG - qB^z)_e = M_e^z > 0$. Thus, any differences in domestic policy effectiveness under regimes I and III cannot be attributed to this assumption. The sign of $\underline{X}$ then depends on the relative magnitudes of α^* and $\beta^*\eta^*$:

$$\underline{X} \gtreqless 0 \quad \text{as} \quad \alpha^* \gtreqless \beta\eta^*. \tag{5.52}$$

Open-market operations: In the absence of an interest-rate target, purchase of domestic bonds for domestic currency by the treasury leads to an increase in both the exchange rate and the demand for labor and a decrease in the interest rate. However, when the central bank is committed to maintaining the current interest rate, its demands for foreign currency and domestic currency reflect that resulting bond ration. Thus, any change in the bond ration will have spillover effects on the foreign-exchange market. The net effects on the exchange rate and bond ration depend on the domestic central bank's elasticity of demand for foreign currency with respect to the bond ration η^* and the relative shares of bonds and foreign currency in its portfolio β^*:

$$de/dM^g = (-m_b^d)\underline{X}^{-1} \tag{5.53}$$

and

$$db/dM^g = (m^f + m^d + T)_e\underline{X}^{-1}, \tag{5.54}$$

with sign $(\underline{X})$ = sign $(\alpha^* - \beta^*\eta^*)$.

If $\beta^*\eta^*$ is greater (less) than α^*, then $\underline{X}$ is negative (positive), and the increase in the stock of domestic currency leads to an exchange-rate depreciation (appreciation) and an increase (decrease) in the central bank's bond ration. Given that the firm has a notional demand for labor and that the interest rate is held constant, the depreciation (appreciation) of the exchange rate leads to an increased (reduced) demand for labor as the firm reduces its demand for the relatively more expensive factor of production.

Fiscal policy: In the absence of an interest-rate target, an increase in the treasury's purchases of goods financed by issuing bonds leads to an increase in the exchange rate and a decrease in the bond price. In this case, the effect on employment was shown to be ambiguous (see regime I of this chapter). However, as in the case of open-market operations, targeting the interest rate will have spillover effects on the foreign-exchange market. Again, the net effects on the exchange rate and the central bank's bond ration depend on the domestic central bank's elasticity of demand for foreign currency with respect to the bond ration η^* and the relative shares of foreign currency and domestic bonds in its current portfolio β^*:

$$de/dG = q(1 - \beta^*\eta^*)\underline{X}^{-1}, \tag{5.55}$$

$$db/dG = [-e(m^f + \dot{m}^d + T)_e$$
$$+ (eG - q\ddot{B} - qB^* - qB^f)_e]\underline{X}^{-1}. \tag{5.56}$$

If $\alpha^* > \beta^*\eta^* > 1$, then $(1 - \beta^*\eta^*) < 0$ but $\underline{X} > 0$; so the exchange rate appreciates, and the bond ration increases. On the other hand, if $\beta^*\eta^* > \alpha^* > 1$, then $(1 - \beta^*\eta^*) < 0$ and $\underline{X} < 0$; so the exchange rate depreciates, and the bond ration decreases. With the firm substituting the relatively cheaper input for the relatively more expensive input, the depreciation (appreciation) of the domestic currency (with a constant interest rate) leads to an increase (decrease) in the demand for labor.

5.6   Concluding remarks

When the central bank's portfolio selection is constrained by its stabilization policies, its demands for assets are effective demands. This is due to the fact that when an asset price is being stabilized, the quantity of that asset in the portfolio of the central bank is the negative of the net excess demand for that asset by other market participants. Thus, price stabilization effectively imposes a quantity ration on the central bank's portfolio choice, and asset markets become interdependent through quantities in addition to prices. Thus, the treasury's policies that alter the central bank's asset ration will have spillover effects on markets for non-rationed assets. Through this channel (spillovers), the effects of the treasury's policies can be altered qualitatively. It was demonstrated that the magnitude of the spillover effects depends on the central bank's elasticities of demand for the non-rationed assets with respect to the quantity of the rationed asset and the relative shares of assets in the central bank's portfolio.

This chapter, by highlighting the potential qualitative change in the effects of the treasury's policies due to the portfolio selection of the central bank (spillover effects in asset markets), points out additional relevant variables that should be taken into account for correct policy prescriptions.

CHAPTER 6

Summary

This chapter discusses the results in Chapters 2 to 5. Section 6.1 surveys Chapters 2 to 4. The results in Chapter 5 are reviewed in section 6.2.

6.1   Chapters 2–4

6.1.1   Bond-financed increase in government spending

In Chapter 2 (regime I), the firm was rationed in the credit market, and the household was rationed in the labor market. In this environment, a bond-financed increase in government spending further crowds out the firm from the credit market, which leads to a reduction in planned production and thus a decrease in both inventory accumulation and the demand for labor. The reduction in the demand for goods used as input increases the current supply of goods, which improves the balance of trade. As labor demand decreases, the household's labor income is reduced. In response to this, the household reduces its demand for goods and assets (money and bonds). The decrease in the demand for bonds further reduces the firm's bond ration, causing another round of cutbacks in planned production. Thus, in this regime, the interdependence of the markets through quantity rations introduces a multiplier process that reduces planned production in each round. However, it was shown that the expansionary effect of the increase in government spending exceeds the contractionary effect of the reduced bond ration; so the net effect is a deterioration in the balance of trade.

In Chapter 3 (regime II), the household was rationed in the bond and labor markets, but the firm was not rationed in any market. In this environment, the firm's demands are notional demands. Notional demands are independent of quantity rations. Thus, an increase in government spending (with rigid prices) has no effect on the demand for labor and the current supply of goods. The increase in the stock of bonds that accompanied the increase in government spending reduces the household's credit ration. In response to this, the household reduces its demand for goods, which improves the balance of trade. However, as long as the marginal propensity to consume out of disposable wealth is

Table 6.1. *Effects of a policy of bond-financed increase in government spending*

Area affected	Regime I[a]	Regime II[b]	Regime III[c]
Employment (− denotes decrease)	−	0	−
Balance of trade (+ denotes deterioration)	+	+	+

[a] Regime I: Firms rationed in the credit market.
[b] Regime II: Households rationed in the credit market.
[c] Regime III: Households and firms rationed in the credit market.

less than one, the decrease in consumption demand will be less than the increase in government spending; so the net effect is a deterioration of the balance of trade.

In Chapter 4 (regime III), the household was rationed simultaneously in the bond and labor markets, whereas the firm was rationed only in the bond market. The increase in government spending leads to a decrease in the demand for labor (as in Chapter 2). However, there is no multiplier process because the allocation of the stock of bonds is fixed. The multiplier process in regime I was a consequence of an endogenous bond ration. Again, the direct effect of an increase in government purchases exceeds the contractionary effects of the decrease in the household's and the firm's bond rations; so the net effect is a deterioration of the balance of trade.

Table 6.1 summarizes the results just discussed. It is clear that the impact of fiscal policy on unemployment and the balance of trade is conditioned in part by the nature of rationing in the credit market. Fiscal policy is an effective instrument for improving internal and external balances under regimes I and III, though it can affect only the external balance in regime II.

6.1.2   Open-market purchases of bonds

When firms are rationed in the credit market (as in regimes I and III) an expansionary monetary policy leads to higher employment and worsens the balance of trade. However, the transmission mechanism is different across these regimes.

In regime I, the firm is rationed only in the credit market, and the household is rationed only in the labor market. In this environment, an open-market purchase of bonds increases the firm's credit ration (its disposable wealth increases), which leads to an increase in planned production. As planned production increases, the firm's demands for

Table 6.2. *Effects of a policy of open-market purchases of bonds*

Area affected	Regime I[a]	Regime II[b]	Regime III[c]
Employment (+ denotes increase)	+	0	+
Balance of trade (+ denotes deterioration)	+	+	+

[a] Regime I: Firms rationed in the credit market.
[b] Regime II: Households rationed in the credit market.
[c] Regime III: Firms and households rationed in the credit market.

inputs increase; thus, employment increases, and the current supply of goods decreases. The increase in employment feeds back on the bond market in terms of an increase in the demand for bonds by the household. Here the multiplier process begins, causing an increase in the level of employment and a deterioration of the balance of trade in each round.

In regime III, the firm is rationed in the credit market, and the household is rationed simultaneously in the bond and labor markets. In this environment, an expansionary monetary policy leads to an increase in the demand for labor and a deterioration of the balance of trade. The transmission mechanism differs from that in regime I in two respects. First, the exogeneity of the supply of loanable funds eliminates the multiplier process, which reduces the impact on employment and the balance of trade. Second, the increase in the household's disposable wealth leads to an increase in consumption demand, which worsens the balance of trade.

In regime II, the firm has notional demands for goods (i.e., the firm is not rationed in any market), and the household has effective demands for goods that reflect its rations in the bond and labor markets. In this environment, an expansionary monetary policy has no impact on the firm's demand functions (as long as prices are rigid). The only impact of this policy is on the demand for goods and, hence, on the balance of trade. As the household's disposable wealth increases, its demands for goods increases, which worsens the balance of trade.

In regimes I and II, an expansionary monetary policy cannot bring about simultaneous improvement in internal and external balances because this monetary policy increases employment but worsens the balance of trade. In regime II, monetary policy has no impact on employment. An improvement in the balance of trade, under regime II, can be achieved with a contractionary monetary policy. Table 6.2 summarizes the results of expansionary monetary policy. It is notable that, under regimes I and II, expansionary monetary and fiscal policies affect the internal balance differently: The former improves the internal balance, and the latter worsens it.

6.1.3 Devaluation

In macroeconomic models, devaluation sometimes is treated independently of the budget constraint. The results of these models should be viewed with caution because the treasury's budget constraint requires that a devaluation of the domestic currency be accompanied by a change in the stock of money, the stock of bonds, real government purchases, or the interest rate (or a change in net taxes when net taxes are not zero). In the preceding chapters, the impact of devaluation on the balance of trade was shown to be conditional on the relative size of direct and spillover effects; thus, in general, the impact is ambiguous. However, the results suggest that the method of financing the devaluation can alter its impact on employment and the balance of trade quantitatively and potentially qualitatively. Because the results obtained, in terms of the relative impact of alternative methods of financing a devaluation on the balance of trade, are fairly uniform across all regimes, only a summary of the results of devaluation under regime III is presented in this section.

The transmission mechanism of a money-financed devaluation for the regimes considered is simpler than other forms of devaluation. For this reason the effectiveness of the alternative means of financing a devaluation are compared with that of a money-financed devaluation.

When there is unemployment and a general excess demand for credit, a money-financed devaluation of the domestic currency leads to an increase in the demand for labor as the firm substitutes the relatively cheap labor input for goods input. With the lower demand for goods as input, the current supply of goods increases. These are the direct effects of a money-financed devaluation (denoted D_e). In addition, there is a spillover effect (denoted S_e) due to the increase in employment. As employment increases, the household's demand for goods increases (wealth effect), which worsens the balance of trade.

If instead of an increase in the stock of money, the government reduces its purchases, the likelihood of an improvement in the balance of trade increases; this is due to the direct effect of the decrease in government purchases on the balance of trade (denoted D_G), which improves it. The effect on employment is the same as in the case of money-financed devaluation because the household's and the firm's disposable wealth are not affected by either policy.

If devaluation is financed by increasing the stock of domestic bonds, its effect on employment is uncertain because the increase in the supply of bonds crowds out the firm from the credit market. In response to this, the firm reduces its demand for inputs, causing a decrease in the level of employment and an increase in the current supply of goods. The decrease in the demand for labor that is due to the reduction in the firm's disposable wealth may offset the increase in demand for labor that is due to the substitution effect. Thus, the net effect on employment is uncertain. In addition to the direct and spillover effects of a money-financed devaluation (i.e., D_e and S_e), there is (1) the direct effect of the reduction in the firm's disposable wealth on the demand for goods as input (denoted D_B), which improves the balance of trade by increasing the current supply of goods, and (2) the spillover effect of the reduction in employment due to the firm's reduced disposable wealth (denoted S_B), which improves the balance of trade by reducing the household's labor income and thus its demand for goods. Therefore, a bond-financed devaluation is more likely to improve the balance of trade than a money-financed devaluation. However, a bond-financed devaluation may lead to lower employment.

Finally, the government can reduce the bond price to accommodate a devaluation (for the regime under consideration, the government is a net buyer of bonds). In this case, the firm's and the household's disposable wealth are again reduced and for the same reasons as in the case of a bond-financed devaluation (discussed earlier), the net effect on employment is uncertain, whereas the likelihood of an improvement in the balance of trade is greater than in the case of a money-financed devaluation. These results are summarized in Table 6.3, where D_q and S_q denote the direct and spillover effects of a decrease in the bond price on the balance of trade.

6.1.4 Decrease in the real wage

In macroeconomic models existence of unemployment is often explained in terms of downward rigidity of the nominal wage (i.e., too high a real wage). The results of regimes II and III were consistent with this view (see Table 6.4). However, in regime I, the relationship between the real wage and employment was shown to be conditional on the relative magnitudes of the direct and spillover effects of a change in the real wage.

In regime II, the firm has notional demands. In this environment, a decrease in the real wage (i.e., a decrease in the nominal wage with a fixed exchange rate) leads to a substitution of the relatively cheaper labor input for goods input, causing an increase in the level of employment.

Table 6.3. *Effects of alternative methods of financing a devaluation*

Method	Effect on employment (+ denotes increase)	Effect on balance of trade[a] (+ denotes deterioration)
Increase in stock of money	+	$\bar{D}_e + \overset{+}{S}_e$
Decrease in government purchases	+	$\bar{D}_e + \bar{D}_G + \overset{+}{S}_e$
Increase in stock of bonds	?	$\bar{D}_e + \bar{D}_B + \overset{+}{S}_e + \bar{S}_B$
Decrease in bond price	?	$\bar{D}_e + \bar{D}_q + \overset{+}{S}_e + \bar{S}_q$

Note: All results are for regime III, in which the household is rationed in the bond and labor markets, while the firm is rationed only in the bond market.

[a] D_x and S_x denote, respectively, direct and spillover effects of a change in the policy instrument x; e denotes the exchange rate (i.e., domestic price of foreign currency); G is real government spending; B is bonds; and q is the domestic nominal price of bonds.

Table 6.4. *Effects of a policy of decrease in the real wage*

Area affected	Regime I[a]	Regime II[b]	Regime III[c]
Employment (+ denotes increase)	?	+	+

[a] Regime I: Firms rationed in the credit market.
[b] Regime II: Households rationed in the credit market.
[c] Regime III: Firms and households rationed in the credit market.

In regime III, the firm's demands are effective demands that reflect its bond ration. However, the bond ration is independent of prices. Thus, a decrease in the real wage leads to an increase in the demand for labor (again the substitution effect).

In regime I, the firm is rationed in the bond market, and the household is rationed in the labor market. The firm's bond ration depends on the household's effective demand for bonds, whereas the household's effective demand for bonds depends on the firm's effective demand for labor. In this environment, a reduction in the real wage increases employment due to the substitution of labor for goods, but the reduction in the real wage and the increase in the household's labor ration feed back on the labor market via their effect on the firm's bond ration, making the net effect on employment uncertain.

All the results of a change in the real wage should be viewed with caution because, in general, a change in the real wage (with a fixed exchange rate) affects the treasury's budget constraint through its effect on taxes. The way in which the treasury accommodates these changes determines the effect of a change in the real wage on employment. The assumption in the preceding chapters has been that net taxes are zero.

6.1.5   Increase in the firm's share of the existing stock of credit

When there is general excess demand for credit, the government can increase the level of employment by reallocating the stock of credit. An increase in the firm's share of the existing stock of credit increases the firm's disposable wealth and so leads to an increased demand for factors of production. As the demand for goods used as input increases, the current supply of goods decreases, which worsens the balance of trade. The increase in employment increases consumption demand, while the decrease in the household's disposable wealth reduces it. Thus, the net effect on the balance of trade is ambiguous.

6.2   Chapter 5

6.2.1   Monetary and fiscal policies

In Chapter 5 (regime I), households are rationed as sellers in the labor market. The central banks and the firms are not rationed in any market. In this case, an open market purchase of bonds results in a higher bond price. A change in the bond price alters both the transactions and speculative demand for foreign currency. The increase in the bond price affects consumption demand both directly and through its effect on the labor ration. When the direct effect of the increase in the bond price on consumption dominates its spillover effect, consumption demand increases. Firms have a notional supply of goods, and so the increase in the bond price decreases the current supply of goods. Both the increased consumption demand and the reduced supply of goods lead to an increased transactions demand for foreign currency. The increase in the bond price also leads to portfolio substitution by the central banks. Thus, the net effect is an excess demand for foreign currency, which leads to exchange rate depreciation. The final effect is a higher exchange rate and a higher bond price, both of which increase the level of employment.

In regime I, an increase in the treasury's purchases of goods financed by issuing bonds leads to a lower bond price. The reduction in the bond price leads to a substitution of bonds for currencies in portfolios. This

Table 6.5. *Macroeconomic effects of the treasury's policies under managed floating exchange-rate and interest-rate regimes*

Regime	Change in prices and rations[a]		
I^b	n	e	q
$dG = 0, dM^g > 0$	+	+	+
$dG > 0, dM^g = 0$	?	+	−
II^c	n	m	q
$dG = 0, dM^g > 0$			
$\beta\eta < \alpha$	+	−	+
$\beta\eta > \alpha$	−	+	−
$dG > 0, dM^g = 0$			
$\alpha > \beta\eta > 1$	+	−	+
$\beta\eta > \alpha > 1$	−	+	−
III^d	n	e	b
$dG = 0, dM^g > 0$			
$\beta^*\eta^* < \alpha^*$	−	−	−
$\beta^*\eta^* > \alpha^*$	+	+	+
$dG > 0, dM^g = 0$			
$\beta^*\eta^* > \alpha^* > 1$	+	+	−
$\alpha^* > \beta^*\eta^* > 1$	−	−	+

Note: In this table,

$$\beta \equiv q\tilde{B}^d/em;$$
$$\eta \equiv -(m/\tilde{B}^d)\tilde{B}^d_m;$$
$$\alpha \equiv [(qB^g_o - q\tilde{B}^z)_q]/[(em^f + eT)_q];$$
$$\beta^* \equiv e\dot{m}^d/qb;$$
$$\eta^* \equiv -(b/\dot{m}^d)(\dot{m}^d_b); \text{ and}$$
$$\alpha^* \equiv [-e(m^f + \dot{m}^d + T)_e]/[(eG - q\ddot{B} - qB^* - qB^f)_e].$$

$(.)_x$ denotes the partial derivative of the variables in parentheses with respect to x; G is real government spending; M^g, the stock of domestic money; q, the bond price (inverse of the interest rate); e, the domestic price of foreign currency (i.e., the exchange rate); n, the household's labor ration; m, the domestic central bank's foreign-currency ration; b, the domestic central bank's bond ration; $\tilde{B}^d$, the domestic central bank's effective demand for bonds; B^g_o, the initial stock of bonds; $\tilde{B}^z$, the aggregate demand for bonds; T, the balance of trade (domestic aggregate demand minus domestic aggregate supply); m^f, the foreign central bank's demand for foreign currency; $\dot{m}^d$, the domestic central bank's effective demand for foreign currency; $\ddot{B}$, the household's effective demand for bonds; B^*, the firm's demand for bonds; and B^f, the foreign central bank's demand for bonds.

[a] + denotes increase; − denotes decrease.

[b] Regime I: No rationing in the asset markets.

[c] Regime II: Domestic central bank rationed in the foreign-exchange market.

[d] Regime III: Domestic central bank rationed in the bond market.

decrease in the bond price also leads, through its effect on consumption demand and current supply of goods, to a decrease in the transactions demand for foreign currency. However, the increase in the treasury's real purchases increases the transactions demand for foreign currency. The net effect is an increased demand for foreign currency which leads to an exchange rate depreciation. An exchange rate depreciation leads to a substitution of bonds and money for foreign currency, which reduces somewhat the decrease in the bond price. The exchange rate depreciation also increases the demand for labor, but the reduction in the bond price decreases employment. Thus, the net effect on employment depends on the relative magnitude of the exchange rate and interest rate effects.

In regimes II and III, the domestic central bank is rationed in the foreign exchange market and the bond market respectively. The households are rationed in the labor market; the foreign central bank and the domestic firms are not rationed in any market. The domestic central bank's ration is due to the conflict between its primary objective (price stabilization) and its portfolio selection. The central bank's demands for assets are effective demands when its portfolio selection is constrained by its stabilization policies. This is because during asset price stabilization, the quantity of that asset in the portfolios of the central bank is the negative of the net excess demand for that asset by other market participants. In effect, price stabilization imposes a quantity ration on the central bank's portfolio choice. This quantity ration makes asset markets interdependent through quantities as well as prices. Thus, those treasury policies that alter the central bank's asset ration will have spillover effects on markets for the non-rationed assets. Through such spillovers, the effects of the treasury's policies can be altered qualitatively. (See Table 6.5 for a summary of the results.) The magnitude of the spillover effects depends on the central bank's elasticities of demand for the non-rationed assets with respect to the quantity of the rationed asset, and on the relative shares of assets in the central bank's portfolio.

The spillover effects in asset markets (the central bank's portfolio selection) can alter qualitatively the effects of treasury policies. Thus, these spillover effects must be taken into account in designing macroeconomic policy.

Appendix: Monetary and fiscal policies with a flexible interest rate

In Chapters 2 to 4, it was demonstrated that when the firm is rationed in the credit market, expansionary monetary policy leads to higher employment, whereas an expansionary fiscal policy reduces it. In this appendix, the differential effects of monetary and fiscal policies on employment are highlighted once again. Here, the interest rate is flexible. Section A.1 reviews the basic model; section A.2 discusses the comparative static results.

A.1   The model

The small, open economy produces a traded-composite good by employing domestic labor and previously produced goods. The domestic economic agents are the household, the firm, the treasury, and the central bank. The goods are labor, produced goods, domestic money, domestic bonds, and foreign money. There is no capital mobility.

The behavior of domestic economic agents is discussed below.

The treasury's purchases of goods are financed by issuing domestic assets (money and bonds). The central bank holds sufficient foreign currency reserves to maintain the exchange rate e. The households are rationed only in the labor market. The firms are not rationed in any market.

The domestic nominal wage w and the foreign nominal price of goods p^* are rigid in the short run. However, the domestic nominal bond price q is flexible in the short run. Purchasing-power parity and a rigid world price of goods, normalized to one, imply that the exchange rate e is the domestic nominal price of goods.

The behavior of the households and the firms was discussed in detail in section 2.3 and 2.4. The treasury's budget constraint is the same as in section 2.2.

A.2   Comparative statics

The domestic economy is in a temporary equilibrium with excess supply of labor when the behavior of all agents is mutally consistent with each other. In particular, the equilibrium of this regime requires that the domestic firm, based on current prices, regenerates the household's labor supply ration. This equilibrium is characterized by A.1 and A.2.

$$E^*(\dot{e}, \dot{w}, \dot{q}) = n \tag{A.1}$$

$$B^*(\dot{e}, \dot{w}, \bar{q}) + \tilde{B}(\dot{e}, \dot{w}, \bar{q}, \dot{n}) = B^g \tag{A.2}$$

Where E^* is the firm's notional demand for labor, n is the labor ration, B^* is the firm's notional demand for bonds, $\tilde{B}$ is the household's effective demand for bonds, and B^g is the stock of government bonds. The balance of trade T in real units is:

$$T = \tilde{C}(\bar{e}, \dot{w}, \dot{q}, \dot{n}) + G - Y^*(\dot{e}, \dot{w}, \bar{q}), \tag{A.3}$$

where $\tilde{C}$ is the effective consumption demand, G is real government consumption, and Y^* is the notional current supply of goods.

Replacing B^g with $\tilde{B}(e, w, q, n) + B^*(e, w, q)$ in government budget constraint yields:

$$eG = M^g - M_o^g + q\tilde{B}(e, w, q, n) + qB^*(e, w, q) - (q + 1)B_o^g. \tag{A.4}$$

To examine the effect of a change in government spending G and money supply M^g on employment n, the balance of trade T, and the bond price q, totally differentiate (A.1), (A.3), and (A.4):

$$\begin{bmatrix} -E_q^* & 1 & 0 \\ Y_q^* - \tilde{C}_q & -\tilde{C}_n & 1 \\ \tilde{B} + B^* + q\tilde{B}_q + qB_q^* - B_o^g & q\tilde{B}_n & 0 \end{bmatrix} \begin{bmatrix} dq \\ dn \\ dT \end{bmatrix} = \begin{bmatrix} 0 \\ dG \\ e\,dG - dM^g \end{bmatrix}. \tag{A.5}$$

The determinant A^{-1} of the matrix of the coefficients is

$$A^{-1} = \tilde{B} + B^* + q\tilde{B}_q + qB_q^* + q\tilde{B}_n E_q^* - B_o^g$$
$$= (q\tilde{B} + qB^* - (q + 1)B_o^g)_q, \tag{A.6}$$

where $(.)_x$ denotes the partial derivative of the variable in parentheses with respect to x.

To sign the determinant, rewrite the budget constraint of the household and the firm to obtain

$$q\tilde{B} - (q + 1)B_o = -e\tilde{C} - \tilde{M} + M_o + wn \tag{A.7}$$

and

$$qB^* - (q + 1)B_o^* = eY^* - M^* + M_o^* - wE^*. \tag{A.8}$$

Next, add (A.7) and (A.8), and let $n = E^*$ to obtain

$$q\tilde{B} + qB^* - (q + 1)B_o^g = -e\tilde{C} - \tilde{M} - M^* + eY^* + M_o^g. \tag{A.9}$$

Finally, substitute from (A.9) into (A.6) to obtain

$$A^{-1} = (-e\tilde{C} - \tilde{M} - M^* + eY^* + M_o^g)_q,$$

or $\quad A^{-1} = -e\tilde{C}_q^{\pm} - e\tilde{C}_n\dot{E}_q^* - \tilde{M}_q^{\pm} - \tilde{M}_n\dot{E}_q^* - M_q^{*+} + e\bar{Y}_q^* < 0.$
$$\tag{A.10}$$

A.3 Fiscal policy

A bond-financed increase in government spending (i.e., $dG > 0$ and $dM^g = de = 0$) leads to a higher interest rate as the government offers a lower bond price.

$$dq/dG = \bar{A}e < 0. \tag{A.11}$$

The lower bond price leads the firm to substitute bonds for planned production, reducing its demand for both labor and goods as inputs.

$$dn/dG = \bar{A}\dot{E}_q^{*+}e < 0,$$

and

$$dI^*/dG = I_q^*(dq/dG) = (\dot{I}_q^{*+})\bar{A}e < 0. \tag{A.12}$$

The increase in government purchases worsens the balance of trade directly, whereas the increase in the current supply of goods in conjunction with lower consumption (due to lower employment) improves it. However, it will be shown that the net effect is a deterioration of the balance of trade.

$$dT/dG = A(A^{-1} + e\tilde{C}_nE_q^* + e\tilde{C}_q - eY_q^*). \tag{A.13}$$

Substituting from (A.10) for A^{-1} into (A.13) yields

$$dT/dG = \bar{A}(-\tilde{M}_q^{+} - M_q^{*+} - \tilde{M}_n\dot{E}_q^{*+}) > 0. \tag{A.14}$$

A.4 Monetary policy

An expansionary monetary policy (i.e., $dM^g > 0$ and $de = dG = 0$) leads to a lower interest rate as the bond price is bid up.

$$dq/dM^g = -\bar{A} > 0. \tag{A.15}$$

The increase in the bond price leads to substitution of planned production and domestic currency for bonds and thus leads to an increase in the demand for both labor and goods as inputs.

Table A.1. *Macroeconomic effects of the treasury's policies with a flexible interest rate*

	Endogenous variable		
Policy	Bond price (+ denotes increase)	Employment (+ denotes increase)	Balance of trade (+ denotes deterioration)
Fiscal policy $dG > 0$ and $dM^g = de = 0$	−	−	+
Monetary policy $dM^g > 0$ and $dG = de = 0$	+	+	+

Note: G is real government spending; M^g is the stock of domestic money; and e is the domestic price of foreign currency (i.e., the exchange rate). The interest rate is the inverse of the bond price.

$$dn/dM^g = -\bar{A}\overset{+}{E}_q^* > 0, \qquad (A.16)$$

and

$$dI^*/dM^g = I_q^*(dq/dM) = \overset{+}{I}_q^*(-\bar{A}) > 0. \qquad (A.17)$$

The higher bond price leads to a higher consumption demand via two channels. The household substitutes goods and domestic currency for bonds. This in combination with higher labor income due to higher employment leads to a net increase in consumption demand, which worsens the balance of trade. The increase in the demand for goods used as inputs decreases the current supply of goods, which leads to a further deterioration of the balance of trade.

$$dT/dM^g = (-\overset{+}{E}_q^*\overset{+}{C}_n + \bar{Y}_q^* - \overset{+}{\tilde{C}}_q)\bar{A} > 0. \qquad (A.18)$$

For the regime considered here, an expansionary monetary policy increases the level of employment, whereas an expansionary fiscal policy reduces it (see Table A.1). Here, the results are similar to those in Chapters 2 and 4 where the firm was rationed in the bond market.

Selected bibliography

The reader may find the author's two recent papers of particular interest (Amos 1987 and 1988). These papers apply a version of the models discussed in this book to an economic analysis of the national debt. My current research agenda includes both empirical and theoretical extensions of the models presented here. In particular, I am currently working on two research projects: (1) a macro-econometric model of the U.S. economy and its major trading partners; (2) further development of the model of central bank and treasury behavior and its empirical estimation.

Amos, M., "Expectations, Rationing and the Short Run Equilibrium of a Small Open Economy," unpublished manuscript, 1981.

Amos, M., "Central Bank Portfolio Selection and Stabilization Policies in an Open Economy with Price Rigidities," unpublished manuscript, 1982.

Amos, M., "Macroeconomic Policy Analysis for an Open Economy With Quantity Constraint," unpublished manuscript, copyright 1983.

Amos, M., "Commercial Bank Portfolio Selection and Banking Policies," unpublished manuscript, 1986.

Amos, M., "Macroeconomic Effects of Policies which Reduce the National Debt," unpublished manuscript, 1987.

Amos, M., "The Effects of Taxes on the National Debt: Some Preliminary Results," unpublished manuscript, 1988.

Amos, M., "A Non-Walrasian Macroeconometric Model of the U.S. Economy," in preparation.

Amos, M., "A Model of Central Bank and Treasury Behavior," in preparation.

Barro, R. J., and H. I. Grossman, "A General Disequilibrium Model of Income and Employment," *American Economic Review*, 61 (1971), 82–93.

Barro, R. J., and H. I. Grossman, *Money, Employment and Inflation*. New York and Cambridge: Cambridge University Press, 1976.

Benassy, J.-P., *Disequilibrium Theory*. Berkeley: University of California, Ph.D. Dissertation (unpublished), 1973.

Benassy, J.-P., *The Economics of Disequilibrium*. New York: Academic Press, 1982.

Benassy, J.-P., "Tariffs and Pareto Optimality in International Trade: The Case of Unemployment," *European Economic Review*, 26 (1984), 261–76.

Bohm, V. and P. Levine, "Temporary Equilibria with Quantity Rationing," *Review of Economic Studies*, 46 (1979), 361–78.

Bohm, V., "Prices and Wages in a Simple Macroeconomic Disequilibrium Model," unpublished manuscript, 1981.

Clower, R. W., "The Keynesian Counter-Revolution: A Theoretical Appraisal," in *The Theory of Interest Rates*, ed. by F. M. Hahn and F. P. R. Brechling. London: Macmillan, 1965.

Cuddington, J. T., P. O. Johansson and K. G. Lofgren, *Disequilibrium Macroeconomics in Open Economies*. Oxford: Basil Blackwell, 1984.

Cuddington, J. T. and P. O. Johansson, "Fiscal Deficit Reduction Programs in Developing Countries: Stabilization versus Growth in the Presence of Credit Rationing," unpublished manuscript, 1986.

Dixit, A., "The Balance of Trade in a Model of Temporary Equilibrium with Rationing," *Review of Economic Studies*, 45 (1978), 393–404.

Dixit, A., and V. D. Norman, *Theory of International Trade*. Cambridge: Cambridge University Press, 1980.

Drazen, A., "Recent Developments in Macroeconomic Disequilibrium Theory," *Econometrica*, 48 (1980), 283–306.

Drèze, J., "Existence of an Equilibrium under Price Rigidity and Quantity Rationing," *International Economic Review*, 16 (1975), 301–20.

Fair, R. C., *Specification, Estimation and Analysis of Macroeconomic Models*. Cambridge: Harvard University Press, 1984.

Fitoussi, J. P., *Modern Macroeconomic Theory*. Totowa: Barnes and Noble Imports, 1983.

Gale, D., *Money: In Disequilibrium*. New York: Cambridge University Press, 1983.

Glustoff, E., "On the Existence of a Keynesian Equilibrium," *Review of Economic Studies*, 35 (1968), 327–34.

Grandmont, J.-M. and G. Laroque, "On Temporary Keynesian Equilibria," *Review of Economic Studies*, 43 (1976), 53–67.

Grandmont, J.-M., "Temporary General Equilibrium Theory," *Econometrica*, 45 (1977), 535–72.

Grandmont, J.-M., G. Laroque and Y. Younès, "Equilibrium with Quantity Rationing and Recontracting," *Journal of Economic Theory*, 19 (1978), 84–102.

Green, J. and J.-J. Laffont, "Disequilibrium Dynamics with Inventories and Anticipatory Price-setting," *European Economic Review* 16 (1981), 199–221.

Hahn, F., "Exercises in Conjectural Equilibria," *Scandinavian Journal of Economics*, 79 (1977), 210–26.

Hahn, F. "On Non-Walrasian Equilibria," *Review of Economic Studies*, 45 (1978), 1–18.

Hicks, J. R., *Value and Capital*, 2nd ed. Oxford: Clarendon Press, 1946.

Hildenbrand, K. and W. Hildenbrand, "On Keynesian Equilibria with Unemployment and Quantity Rationing," *Journal of Economic Theory*, 18 (1978), 255–76.

Hool, B., "Monetary and Fiscal Policies in Short Run Equilibria with Rationing," *International Economic Review*, 21 (1980), 301–15.

Hool, B., and J. D. Richardson, "International Trade, Indebtedness and Welfare Repercussions Among Supply Constrained Economies Under Floating Exchange Rates," National Bureau of Economic Research, Working Paper, 571 (1982), Boston.

Keynes, J. M., *The General Theory of Employment, Interest and Money*. New York: Macmillan, 1936.

Laffont, J.-J., "Fix-Price Models: A Survey of Recent Empirical Work," in *Frontiers of Economics*, ed. by Arrow, K. J. and S. Honkapohja. Oxford: Basil Blackwell, 1985.

Leijonhufvud, A., "Keynes and the Keynesians: A Suggested Interpretation," *American Economic Review*, 57 (1967), 401–410.

Leijonhufvud, A., *On Keynesian Economics and the Economics of Keynes*. New York: Oxford University Press, 1968.

Leijonhufvud, A., *Information and Coordination: Essays in Macroeconomic Theory*. New York: Oxford University Press, 1981.

Liviatan, N., "A Disequilibrium Analysis of the Monetary Trade Model," *Journal of International Economics*, 9 (1979), 355–77.

Lorie, H. R. and J. R. Sheen, "Supply Shocks in a Two-Country World with Wage and Price Rigidities," *Economic Journal*, 92 (1982), 849–67.

Malinvaud, E., *The Theory of Unemployment Reconsidered*. Oxford: Basil Blackwell, 1977.

Malinvaud, E., *Profitability and Unemployment*. Cambridge: Cambridge University Press, 1980.

Muellbauer, J., and R. Portes, "Macroeconomic Models with Quantity Rationing," *Economic Journal*, 88 (1978), 788–821.

Neary, J. P., "Nontraded Goods and the Balance of Trade in a Neo-Keynesian Temporary Equilibrium," *Quarterly Journal of Economics*, 15 (1980), 403–30.

Neary, J. P., and K. W. S. Roberts, "The Theory of Household Behavior under Rationing," *European Economic Review*, 13 (1980), 25–42.

Neary, J. P. and J. E. Stiglitz, "Toward a Reconstruction of Keynesian Economics: Expectations and Constrained Equilibria," *Quarterly Journal of Economics*, 98 (1983), 199–228.

Ohlsson, H., "Cost-Benefit Rules in a Regionalized Disequilibrium Model," *Scandinavian Journal of Economics*, 89 (1987), 165–82.

Owen, R. F., "A Two Country Disequilibrium Model," *Journal of International Economics*, 18 (1985), 339–55.

Patinkin, D., *Money, Interest and Prices*, 1956; 2nd ed. New York: Harper and Row, 1965.

Quandt, R. E., *The Econometrics of Disequilibrium*. New York: Basil Blackwell, 1988.

Sondermann, D., "Temporary Competitive Equilibrium Under Uncertainty," in *Allocation Under Uncertainty: Equilibrium and Optimality*, ed. by J. Dreze. London: Macmillan, 1974.

Steigum, E., "Keynesian and Classical Unemployment in an Open Economy," *Scandinavian Journal of Economics*, 82 (1980), 147–166.

Stiglitz, J. E., and A. Weiss, "Credit Rationing in Markets with Imperfect Information," *American Economic Review*, 71 (1983a), 393–409.

Varian, H. R., "On Persistent Disequilibrium," *Journal of Economic Theory*, 10 (1975), 218–28.

Varian, H. R., "Non-Walrasian Equilibria," *Econometrica*, 45 (1977), 573–90.

Younes, Y., "On the Role of Money in the Process of Exchange and the Existence of a Non-Walrasian Equilibrium," *Review of Economic Studies*, 42 (1975), 489–501.